OIKOS

8 to 15

The World Is Smaller Than You Think

Tom Mercer

Unless otherwise noted, all Scripture quotations are from the New International Version of the Bible, 2011.

8 to 15, The World Is Smaller Than You Think
ISBN Number: 978-0-9840364-0-0

Published by Oikos Books
Victorville, CA 92394

Manufactured in the United States of America.

Dedicated to
Sheryl Lynn

Your love for the people around you is the daily
reminder I need to act like Jesus. Your outward beauty
makes everyone who finds out we're married think
I must be rich. I will always be grateful to God for
graciously dropping me in your oikos. I will always be
in love with you for letting Him.

TABLE OF CONTENTS

ACKNOWLEDGMENTS

To transfer passion from your heart to the printed page is no small undertaking. For me, it has been a profound lesson in ecclesiology to see how the gifts of the Spirit can dovetail together to bring a project such as this to life.

My deep gratitude goes to Dr. Bruce and Christine Wingard for their help in creating the original version of this book *(Oikos, Your World Delivered)*. Their skill in transforming the spoken word to the written word is a thing of beauty.

I am also thankful and humbled to work in such a gifted laboratory of pastoral leadership. Three decades ago, Jack Hamilton chose to befriend me. He has since given me his undying loyalty, providing senior leadership for the ministry staff at HDC. He and the rest of our team have chosen to set aside career and ambition, to simply build an effective and enduring church together. They are my constant encouragement and source of accountability.

Likewise, I am grateful for the logistical support that many within our team have offered specifically to this project. From Tony Mercado's cover design to Matt Curtis' page layout and internal design; from Mary Grace's transcriptions to Josh Bishop's expert advice and constant nagging about excellence.

I also want to thank the HDC church family, who faithfully and patiently let me drill oikos into their hearts each week. It is a blessing to regularly listen to the many oikos testimonies that make it clear you've taken it to heart.

Thanks, too, to my guys in San Diego, my mentor group, who have both let me rant about this theme and have held me accountable to finally finish this project.

When he realized whose son I was, a well-known church leader told me with no hesitation, "Your dad wrote the book on youth ministry in Southern California!" PF was a genuine ministry legend. But I am most grateful for the book both he and my mother wrote on my heart by not only leading me to Jesus, but by showing me what a life of service was supposed to look like.

But my deepest gratitude goes to the most important people in my life, the most important part of my own oikos—my wife, my children and my grandchildren. Thank you for giving me so many great reasons to get up every morning!

PROLOGUE

WELCOME TO THE WAR

Sin kills everything it touches. Every time someone makes a bad decision and lets sin creep in, something dies. Sometimes the death is obscure, like when an opportunity to do something really significant simply wilts away. Sometimes it's more noticeable, like when a promising relationship slowly fades away. Sometimes it's downright tragic, like when someone loses hope, buys a handgun and a human life is thrown away.

Considering all that God had provided him, Adam's failure to protect humanity from its own demise is nothing short of incredible. Scholars continue to debate his rhyme or reason. Did he not understand his representative headship? Was he so in love with Eve that he couldn't bear the thought of losing her, that life outside the Garden with her still seemed better to him than life in Paradise without her? Or was the serpent just that compelling? Whatever the rationale, the implication of that one decision was profound. It killed us all.

The Bible says that Adam's first lousy choice was, for all intents and purposes, a declaration of war against God. It created a perpetual state of enmity, separating the Creator from His creation. Ironic as it seems, Adam's children have been trying to make peace with God ever since.

Every religion begins with the same basic assumptions—that we are guilty before God and that we can do something about it. Every creed frames it differently, but they all boil down to the same tactical objective: "We got ourselves into this mess—and we'll get ourselves out." There are over 10,000 religions in the world with two new ones being added every day. And each of them has a strategy to create a state of détente with God, to somehow sooth His ruffled feathers. But like an underwater oilrig with a systemic malfunction, we still can't find a way to cap the problem. The fracture is too deep.

That's why, when you pick up the morning paper and read what's going on around the world or even around the corner, you can see that humanity is still stuck in a losing battle. The problem has always been a simple one—religion simply cannot work. We cannot outlast an eternal God or out-think an omniscient God or out-muscle an omnipotent God or outrun an omnipresent God. We just can't. Our only hope was that He would show us mercy. Which brings us to why the Gospel is so aptly named.

The Incarnation was essentially a military invasion. And resolutely entrenched behind the Gates of Fort Hades, Satan made his position clear—he would not give up willingly. From Herod the Great to Pontius Pilate, he threw everything he had at Jesus—it just wasn't enough. The war ended on a very difficult but very Good Friday. It may have seemed to onlookers as if He was just hanging there on a cruel cross, forgotten and alone, but that's only the way it seemed. In reality, He was completing the mission He had come to fulfill, slowly prying apart the talons of the enemy, dismantling the grip Satan had on our dead hearts and forcing him to sign for his unconditional surrender. The overwhelming force of the Resurrection sealed the enemy's fate and within a matter of days the POWs began returning home.

Today, most of the people you pass at the mall or sit next to at the ballgame are still fighting in ignorance—trying to either suppress their hard-wired knowledge of God's intentions or to negotiate peace with Him on untenable terms. Don't you think it's time they found out that they don't have to live that way anymore?

Does it bother you that some of your friends may still be fighting a war they cannot win? That at least some of the people you love and regularly do life with are still stuck in their sin? No hope? No peace? Nothing to look forward to but more of the same? The prospect of a loved one eternally separated from God *has* to bother you. If not, then maybe you should read something else. If it doesn't bother you, perhaps you should go get a book on how to blame the traditional church for your problems, or one on how some politician is probably the Antichrist, or one on how the views of a rival denomination are so incredibly inept.

But after all the hype about the church finally emerging has run its course; and after all the arguments over virtually every doctrinal disagreement are done (like that will ever happen); and after all the conferences on reinventing everything that has ever been done in the name of Jesus are over, nothing will have really changed. Your friends will still be stuck in a no-win situation. Still, no hope. Still, no peace. Still, nothing to look forward to but more of the same, because, in spite of our deliberations in the name of Christ, we still will not have really done anything Christian yet.

Being a Christ follower doesn't mean you're theologically right. It doesn't mean you're eternally safe. You may be both, but that's still not what it means—Jesus was both right and safe *before* the Incarnation. He had something else in mind when He made Himself nothing and entered a world so different from the one He'd created. He was on a mission.

Stu Weber reflects, "On a lonely midwinter day, I and a couple hundred other soldiers took a flight across the ocean. Boarding that commercial airliner, we stowed our gear and fastened our seat belts just as we had so many times before. It all seemed so routine. But the next time they opened that door, "routine" vanished like a dream. The sights, sounds, and smells that bombarded our senses were overwhelming. It was a whole new world. It was like nothing we had ever seen before. When that door swung open, heat and humidity rolled over us like a tsunami. Every pore in our bodies seeped sweat. And the smell was something else: a strange brew of jet fuel, sewage, rotting vegetables, and smoke. It exploded in our nostrils. This was Vietnam. It looked like the depiction of a war zone that you might have seen in the movies. But this was no movie. There were no marching bands. No cigar-chomping John Wayne to welcome us. No swaggering George Patton to fill us with courage. No shouts of "Rangers lead the way!" Just a single, somewhat tired GI pointing to a line of waiting buses, engines running. His message was simple: "Welcome to the war." [1]

Whether you like it or not, we were all born behind enemy lines. Whether you know it or not, you live in a warzone. Like our Commander before us, deployment is limited, but so is our mission. And therein lies the message of this book. Let's figure out the best way to accomplish our objective, so we can all go home. Together.

INTRODUCTION

LIVING IN A WORLD WHERE EVERYONE GOES TO CHURCH

I serve as a pastor to a group of people who call themselves High Desert Church. We live in the high desert of Southern California, on the I-15 corridor about halfway between San Diego and Las Vegas. The people who attend HDC are extraordinary. Not because they look different than most people who claim to be Christ followers, but because most of them actually follow Christ—not perfectly, of course, but intentionally, to be sure. There is no way for me to convey the message in this book without invoking the experience I've shared with HDC. They've provided a laboratory-like environment where oikocentric thinking has not just taken root—it's taken over!

I realize an author's first responsibility is to, as they say, "define the audience." That is, the sooner a reader recognizes which audience the author has targeted, the sooner he or she can determine if they're part of it! From the beginning, I was inclined to write to any Christian who wants to make a profound difference in their world. The oikos principle certainly provides momentum to that end and the lion's share of the final product focuses there. But as the process unfolded, I realized how critical HDC's role has been in creating a more ideal environment for worldchange to germinate—and the pastor in me began to seep out. If that confuses anyone, I offer a very sincere apology in advance, but I just cannot separate the role of the local church from the mission of the individual believer. At the least, a book about an oikocentric life and a book about an oikocentric church certainly belong on the same shelf. In this case, they will share the same cover.

FORCED TO CHANGE THE WORLD

We hear a lot about China these days, usually regarding the Chinese economy—but that's not the only thing that's grown over there recently. The church in China has grown at a rate history has never witnessed before. Although public Christian assembly remains either banned or heavily monitored, the house church movement has exploded, with much of the growth now migrating from rural areas into the urban centers of the country. In 1949, when the rest of the world was virtually cut off from the Chinese church, there were an estimated 500,000 baptized Evangelical Chinese believers. Today estimates are as high as 130,000,000. And it's not just China—go ahead and Google the underground church in Iran. They're experiencing unparalleled growth as well. In fact Christianity is growing most rapidly in all of the regions of the world where you would least expect it.

When I heard missionary reports about the oppressed church as a kid, I remember connecting dots between spiritual power and martyrdom. Not being too fond of the idea of oppression, political or otherwise, the idea of Christian ministry actually scared me. If you share that same aversion to prison time, here is some good news—it isn't persecution that generates growth, it's the ministry model that political oppression actually *forces* us to embrace. When the church is forced out of a traditional leader-centered ministry model, where the focus is on the platform ministry of highly gifted leaders, into a more relational oikocentric model, where the focus is on the personal ministry of individual believers, the results are startling. Ask a typical Chinese believer where they go to church and they'll probably tell you the same thing Jesus did—they don't go to church, they *are* the church!

If only we could keep that focus when we're not oppressed! But as governments become more tolerant of Christianity, allowing large assemblies to become the center of church life, our tendency is to shift our focus to leadership gifts, leadership conferences and leadership development strategies—and Christian leaders are tempted to think more about moving up the food chain while parishioners tend to think less about reaching out to non-believers to instead focus on finding the best places to "have their needs met" and "be well fed."

In contrast to those regions where Evangelicalism is growing most rapidly, it is growing in the U.S. by a lethargic 0.8%. Rebecca Barnes and Lindy Lowry's *Up Close Look at Church Attendance in America* reports that "less than 20% of Americans regularly attend church—half of what the pollsters report." [1] Among others, they cite respected sociologists C. Kirk Hadaway and Penny Long Marler, whose research revealed that the actual number of people worshiping each week is closer to 52 million people instead of the pollster-reported 132 million (40%). The reason for the discrepancy is what researchers call "the halo effect"—what people tell pollsters versus what they actually do.

But I am proposing that both the mainline 40% pollsters and the less-optimistic 20% pollsters are both wrong. They're research might be dead on but I still think they're wrong. I believe that virtually 100% of the people in this country attend church every week—because church isn't someplace you go—it's someone you know! So most people, who don't yet know what a personal relationship with God looks like and will not be attending a worship service in any particular church building this weekend, will probably still have the chance to see the power of Jesus demonstrated every single day! They're attendance might not be recorded in a database, but people seldom come to Christ because of a pastor's sermon or a great worship band anyway. Virtually all of us who know Christ made our decision to follow Him through a personal relationship with one or more believers who either demonstrated faith to us or answered our questions or (most likely) both—during the week, over the course of many weeks, but not necessarily on a weekend.

But before we move on, let me get this straight—even with all of our emphasis on church leadership, preaching and vision over the past several decades (to say nothing of our marketing campaigns), we can still only talk two out of every ten Americans into coming into a building once a week to listen to us "annointed" leaders preach, yet ten out of ten Americans are interacting with the church on a daily basis.

Hmmm.

That's certainly not to say that attending a weekend service is unimportant—but if that service is not focused on that most important statistic of all then it certainly has lost any relevance to the church's mission. When people hear about HDC, the immediate assumption is that we are a church for "seekers," but we are not. Neither do we aspire to be the "believers" church many of us grew up in. We're not necessarily looking for seekers or believers—we want "partners." Simply stated, HDC is a support group for worldchangers. So if you also want to change your world, or if you want to partner with others in that great cause, then keep reading because you can do both! And you might be surprised to discover that the world is actually smaller than you think!

oikos *n*, extended household (Gr.)

1. the most natural and common environment for evangelism to occur

2. a group of eight to fifteen people with whom you share life most closely, your sphere of greatest influence

3. the people for whom God wants to prepare you to become an ideal instrument of His grace

4. a microcosm of the world at large, for whom God sent His Son—that all who place their faith in Christ would be delivered from the bondage of sin and enjoy life to the fullest

worldchanger *n*, someone who actively encourages people in their relational world (their oikos) to become Christ followers

oikocentric *adj*, having evaluated purpose through the lense of oikos

PART 1:

CHANGING YOUR PERSPECTIVE

"All great change in America begins at the dinner table."

CHAPTER 1
A NEW PAIR OF GLASSES

It was amazing! A group of four students had grown to more than 300, and in just a few years. The amazing part was that it was our youth group. I was their youth pastor, and yet all that growth had little if anything to do with me. Those young people had taken a simple concept and turned their worlds upside down. A few years later, there we were, ministering to more than 300 kids. But let's back up a bit.

Back in 1979 my Senior Pastor asked me to attend a seminar

with him, one led by Dr. Win Arn. Up until then neither of us had heard much about the word *oikos* let alone the principle behind it. I had been hired by the church because the youth ministry needed a boost. (The first Bible study I led had a grand total of four students in attendance. That's right, four!) It was at Dr. Arn's seminar that I was introduced to the basic principle I'm going to share with you. Of course time and experience have refined its implementation, but its efficiency lies in its pure simplicity.

That seminar lit a fire under me. Up to that point I was hesitant to introduce evangelism to the youth group at all. I remembered my own experience with evangelism as a student and never felt comfortable. So for the first time I began feeling like I could be a strategic part of the Great Commission in a natural, authentic way. My Senior Pastor encouraged me to go for it. I felt like a youth pastor unleashed! Three years later the youth group was on the verge of outgrowing the church. Over 300 students had taken this simple idea seriously and had literally turned our community on its ear.

WHAT DID WE LEARN?

Church leaders often struggle with the ongoing challenge of reaching the next generation, but why is it such a struggle?

Maybe a better question would be, why do so many young people stay away from church? I would propose that people will generally do most anything if they're given a good enough reason. Most young people stay away from church for the same reason most older people stay away from church—they simply haven't been given a compelling reason to go. People need a better reason to attend church than "because it's the right thing to do!" The post-modern world we live in no longer recognizes right and wrong with that level of clarity.

A local church may also be tempted to merely see themselves as a self-perpetuating entity, to invite younger Christians to attend only for the sake of keeping the church from folding up its tent. You can often sense their fear in the conversation— that the ministry they've shared for decades would die on their watch. But is that a good reason to have a church—just to see if we can keep it alive for one more generation?

People young and old need to be challenged to see beyond the preoccupations of a self-absorbed culture and look to change their world. Young people want that. When they first emerge onto the scene, every generation aspires to be worldchangers, that is until society convinces them they can't be and the demands of day-to-day survival crush the dream. Well, guess what? That youth group—those four kids were convinced that they could be worldchangers, at least in their own worlds. And then they did it. And that's the point.

God wants to change the world. And we shouldn't be surpised by that—it's not just a story in the Bible, it's the story *of* the Bible. Unfortunately, most of us are content with a good Sunday sermon, comfortable music and lunch afterward with our friends. Most Christians show little interest in worldchange, much less being actual worldchangers. But a nice comfortable church is not the plan that Jesus, the Head of the Church, laid out. He's building a powerful one!

YOU MEAN THERE IS A PLAN?

Jesus designed, taught, modeled, and then gave His plan to His Church. Our task is to simply read the directions and follow that plan. It has been there all the time. The early church had it. The modern church seems to have lost it. But churches around the world are discovering that the oikos model still works as well now as it did then, and that anyone can participate!

Oikos is not a program. It's not an event. It's not an emphasis. It's actually like a new pair of glasses through which we can see our world the way Jesus did. Now pushing 60, my eyesight continues to falter. I'm not asking for sympathy, just that you'd bring a high powered flashlight to the restaurant and show me the inside of the menu from the other side of the table! Anyway, a few years ago I finally had to do what I had been procrastinating about for years—go see an optometrist. He fitted me with a pair of glasses that for the first time in a long time allowed me to see the world around me with clarity. The funny thing is, until I put them on I didn't realize how really poor my vision had ever so gradually become.

In a spiritual dimension, Dr. Arn was my optometrist. I put on my oikos lenses that day and haven't taken them off since! I read the Scriptures with more clarity, see ministry with a sharper focus and plan my daily schedule with a greater sense of urgency. Now I've become somewhat of a spiritual optometrist myself— helping others see how every believer has the opportunity to be God's instrument in the most effective arena possible—their own circle of relationships.

Here's how it works. God has given each of us, on average, anywhere from eight to fifteen people whom He has supernaturally and strategically placed in our relational worlds. The Greeks used one word to describe this personal world— oikos, or "extended household." This is the world God wants to use each of us to change, our individual world!

God has always utilized the family unit as the primary arena for effective evangelism. But the word "families" in the Bible refers to more than we are used to thinking about when we consider families in today's world.

Hans Walter Wolf describes the family unit in the Old

Testament. "A household usually contained four generations, including men, married women, unmarried daughters, slaves of both sexes, persons without citizenship and 'sojourners,' or resident foreign workers." [1]

Keeping that in mind, consider the following verses about the spiritual dynamic in the centrality of the family in God's plan.

"There, in the presence of the LORD your God, you and your families shall eat and shall rejoice in everything you have put your hand to, because the LORD your God has blessed you." (Deuteronomy 12:7)

"And there rejoice before the LORD your God—you, your sons and daughters, your male and female servants, and the Levites from your towns, who have no allotment or inheritance of their own." (Deuteronomy 12:12)

That same extended family continues to be the focus in the New Testament. The Greek word *oikos* describes that same relational target.

President Ronald Reagan was often referred to as The Great Communicator. He was also a great motivator. His larger than life persona and folksy style transcended ideological walls. He was a master at casting a grand vision for a better world while still clarifying how each of us must focus—what every American could and should contribute to our national destiny. "All great change in America," he said, "begins at the dinner table." [2]

Jesus would agree. In fact, He said it first and even said it often. Further, He has actually set a table for you—a table with anywhere from eight to fifteen chairs around it! Your oikos might include the clerk at the grocery store where you shop every week, the server you talk to at a favorite restaurant or that person you keep running into every day at work. Our oikos comprises different kinds of people, all with different needs, but they've all been supernaturally and strategically placed there for a reason—God wants to demonstrate His love and grace to them all through us. We all have an oikos. Your oikos does not contain the same eight to fifteen people who make up mine. But it is that world, *your* world, that God wants to transform, to bring to Himself through the one common denominator they all share—you!

"He wants Texas back!"

Chapter 2
I CAN DO THIS!

I hear the same thing nearly every time I finish presenting an oikos workshop. Sometimes it's a rookie, fresh out of seminary, excited with the prospects of reinvigorating the church. Sometimes it comes from church volunteers, overwhelmed with their workload and already weary of the prospective "next" program. Sometimes it's from veteran pastors who have tried everything they could get their hands on to involve their church in the Great Commission. But most often it comes from someone who has grown up in church praying that others would somehow do what they don't believe they can—change the world for Christ.

A few years ago I began meeting regularly with a group of pastors in San Diego. As you can imagine, from the very beginning of the group's relationship, the oikos principle bled into every one of our conversations. But one of the guys would look at me sideways every time oikos came up. He just couldn't believe effective ministry could evolve out of such a simple premise. I talked him into attending a workshop anyway, hoping he would come to better understand the principle—at least then he would know what he was rejecting!

After the first part of the presentation was over he walked up to me and said, "I'm sold," as if there was never a doubt! I actually thought he was teasing me—up to that point he had been so resistant it was hard to believe he had done a "180" so quickly. I asked, "What happened?"

"Tom," he said, "it was the weirdest thing. About halfway through your talk, my wife leaned over to me and whispered, 'I can do this!' When she said that, the light went on!"

OIKOS IS A NATURAL

The oikos model is the most natural organizational principle for both the lifestyle of a Christian and the ministry of a local church. Another way to describe oikos is that it is organic. It is totally authentic—there is nothing artificial about it. It's not imported from someone or somewhere else. In fact, it's already at work wherever you attend church, in your home and in your individual life.

It *fits* all ages and levels of maturity.

It *flows* naturally out of a Christian lifestyle.

It *fuels* discipleship like no program can.

It *facilitates* the growth of Christ's church like nothing else.

It *finances* itself.

It is *faithful* to the Bible.

But the oikos model is also simple—and that's important because the spiritual heritage of our salvation is rooted in simplicity.

The warning in the Garden of Eden was simple.

Stay away from just one tree.

The cost of disobedience was simple.

You will die.

The Law's lesson was simple.

We're in trouble.

The plan of redemption is simple.

We can be set free.

The price of redemption was simple.

A perfect Sacrifice.

The message of the cross is simple.

Unconditional love.

The essence of salvation is simple.

Amazing grace.

In baseball lingo those are all fastballs. No junk, nothing sneaky or complicated. Ninety miles an hour, right over the middle of the plate. So when it comes to His strategy for evangelism why would God throw us a hard slider down and away? As I said before, nobody would ever say Christianity is easy, but it has always been simple.

THE VERSE THAT HAUNTS ME THE MOST

"We should not make it difficult for the Gentiles who are turning to God." (Acts 15:19)

There is a context to that statement to be sure, but the essence is clear. The Apostles were like us. Left to their own devices, they tended to make everything more difficult than it should be. The Gospel was just their latest victim.

You would expect that from the Judaizers. Kings of complexity and yet they were Christians. They prided themselves on being more "legal" than anyone, but perfectionism gets complicated. For them it evolved well beyond commitment. They became impossible to please because the Law was impossible to oblige. Nobody could ever accuse them of not trying, but at the end of the day, it was like being declared the Valedictorian of Summer School—who cares?

So, before any further damage could be done, the Apostle Paul called them out. At the first Council of the Christian church, James and the rest of his legal team were forced to deal with what the Gospel really was. Before the day was over, they at least came to grips with what it really wasn't. And what it wasn't was complicated! James' words reflect his concern that he had been part and parcel to the unthinkable—he had actually been making it difficult for non-believers to come to Christ. This was only a few years after the cross and the fire of the church was already being doused by waves of complexity.

WE'VE MET THE ENEMY

Back in 1981, Fernandomania gripped the City of Los Angeles. Dodger fans couldn't get enough of Fernando Valenzuela, a kid from Sonora, Mexico. His efforts made him the odds-on favorite to be the league's top rookie, starting the season 8-0 with five shutouts and an ERA of 0.50. When asked about Valenzuela's contract negotiations, Tommy Lasorda, the longtime Manager of the Dodgers, responded matter-of-factly, "He wants Texas back!"[1] Lasorda had a knack for getting his point across—the kid's payday would certainly be huge.

But as large as it seemed at the time, Fernando's contract was peanuts compared to what players are paid these days! Now a self-aggrandizing web of complex business transactions, litigation, ridiculous contracts and even more ridiculous cable television deals, the simple game we loved to play as kids seems to have lost much of its soul.

Some years ago, I was invited to interview with a publishing company. Its Editor-in-Chief was one of the kindest and godliest men I've ever known. A mutual friend had sent him some of my reflections about the Scriptures. I was encouraged that he believed in me and was honored that his editors would give me some of their valuable time. I walked into the main exhibition hall of the convention center that day and, quite frankly, couldn't believe what I saw. It was the world's largest assemblage of Christian publishers, corporate Christianity at its best. This is not meant as a critical commentary, business is what it is. I met many wonderful people that day, virtually all of them reflecting a sincere desire to do Kingdom work. But, that aside, what impressed me the most was how we had all somehow been sucked into a vortex of complexity.

In what has unfortunately become the competitive and complex world of faith, we have met the enemy—and they are us! While we regularly try to reinvent the church in as many ways as our conferences and seminars can explain, the biblical strategy for changing the world remains constant. The foundation of that strategy is oikos. And what it lacks in creativity it also lacks in complexity. Which, of course, is why even *I can do this!*

"We strayed from the formula and we paid the price!"

OK

Chapter 3
STATISTICALLY SPEAKING

In research, 95% is a statistical anomaly or, as Malcolm Gladwell would designate it, an *outlier*—"a statistical observation that is markedly different in value from the others of the sample." [1]

For example, if medical research revealed that, of all those who experienced remission from cancer, 95% had received the same type of treatment, you better believe that's all the oncology world would be talking about.

Or if a Golf Magazine reporter discovered that, of all of the golfers who had won a tournament championship on the tour over the last twenty years, 95% of them used the same brand of golf ball, it would not only be the cover story, but every other supplier would be breaking down that one ball, trying to figure out what makes it tick.

Or if 95% of the MVP's in all professional sports grew up in your hometown, ESPN would have already been out there testing the water!

Or if 95% of all believers came to Christ through the same ministry model, you'd think that every Christian seminary, magazine and church would be all over it. But if you *did* think that, you'd be advised to think again. That's what amazes me— of all of those who placed their faith in Jesus, from every generation, culture and denomination for the past 2,000 years, it seems that 95% came to Christ primarily through the influence of someone in their oikos, yet many churches essentially dismiss it.

Oikos is an outlier because we naturally have more opportunities to share Christ with those people we are around the most. As a result, our faith can be demonstrated to our oikos in our daily lives, as we're carefully scrutinized on a regular basis by those eight to fifteen people. God is absolutely sold on using your extended household, your oikos, as the natural arena where your testimony can be clearly communicated. We will talk more later about exactly how to determine who is in your oikos and what specifically to do about them, but the idea should not surprise anyone who has read the New Testament.

THE ORIGINAL PLAN

After healing the demon possessed man, Jesus told him specifically to:

"Go home to your own people (oikos) and tell them how much the Lord has done for you, and how he has had mercy on you." (Mark 5:19)

Immediately following Zacchaeus' conversion, Jesus reflected on what had just happened:

"Today salvation has come to this house (oikos)." (Luke 19:9)

When Jesus healed the son of a royal official:

"...he and his whole household (oikos) believed." (John 4:53)

Jesus called Levi (Matthew) to be His disciple:

"While Jesus was having dinner [with] Levi's house (oikos) many tax collectors and sinners were eating with him and his disciples, for there were many who followed him." (Mark 2:15)

In Acts 10 we see the first example of a Gentile oikos coming to Christ. Cornelius responded to the Gospel presentation that Peter made and he and his household became believers. In reporting to the church leaders in Jerusalem, Peter reflected on what the angel had told Cornelius about Peter:

"He will bring you a message through which you and all your household (oikos) will be saved." (Acts 11:14)

The story continued in Philippi with Lydia and the city jailor, both of whom responded to the Apostle Paul's challenge to place their faith in Christ. Acts 16 describes how, in both cases, an oikos believed and were all baptized. And as the Biblical record comes to an end, the same tactical approach to worldchange continues to gain momentum from one century to the next. Our "households" have always been the most natural arenas where our testimonies can be most clearly and powerfully communicated.

A SURPRISING LOOK

Research by Dr. Thom Reiner revealed *"Ten Surprises About the Unchurched."* [2] Over the course of three years, his research team of seventeen men and women took to the streets of America. They covered all fifty states, interviewing a diversity of ethnic groups and socioeconomic groups. Wide-ranging demographic areas were also covered, and as many females as males were interviewed. There were those from a modest education all the way to doctoral degrees. Every person interviewed was deemed to be both unchurched and non-Christian. During those three years, they uncovered some interesting facts.

• Most of the unchurched feel guilty about not attending church. If they feel guilty, then why do they avoid church? Their research revealed that the unchurched do not feel as if they can fit into the protocol of a local church. They feel they will be out of place.

• 96% of the unchurched are at least somewhat likely to attend church if they are invited. 96%! That means, of the 160 million unchurched people in the United States, 154 million of them would be at least somewhat likely to come to church if someone would just invite them—but only 2% of active churchgoers ever do!

• Very few of the unchurched have ever had someone share with them how to become a Christian. In light of the fact that so few people invite an unchurched individual to attend church, it is not a shock to discover that neither do they invite them to know Christ.

• Most of the unchurched have a positive view of pastors and the church. Only a few said they thought that clergy were hypocrites or only after their money. That again was a paradigm shift for me because I had been told that everybody who didn't go to church thought the primary reason I wanted them to come was to tithe. But evidently, according to the research, that is not the case.

• Many of the unchurched have a church background, which tells us that they left church for a reason. And the reason is because many of them attended churches that had no relevance to them—which means if we are going to reach them we may have to rethink the ways we do church.

• Some types of cold calls are effective, but many are not. The definition of a cold call is simply engaging in a conversation to which you have not been invited. One guy they interviewed said, "I don't mind talking to people from churches, but please don't show up at my home without an invitation—it reminds me of a telephone solicitation, only worse."

• The unchurched would like to develop a real and sincere relationship with a Christian. The irony is, virtually all of them have regular relationships with a number of Christians already.

• The attitudes of the unchurched are not correlated to where they live, their ethnic or racial background or their gender. In other words, the same attitudes tend to cross over all of those boundaries.

• Many of the unchurched are far more concerned about the spiritual well being of their children than they are about themselves.

Pulling all of that together, the whole thing looks like a set up! I mean, if the vast majority of people in the U.S. have never had anyone tell them how to become a Christian, yet 96% of the unchurched population would be receptive if someone simply invited them to church, and most non-believers would like to develop a close relationship with a Christ follower...what are we afraid of and what are we waiting for?

WHAT HAPPENED?

When movie studio boss, Harry Flugleman, explained to *The Three Amigos* why their last few movies had been box office flops, he said, in no uncertain terms, "We strayed from the formula and we paid the price!"[3] What's not so funny is that, over the course of the last Century we've done the same thing—we've unwittingly, yet gradually allowed Jesus' formula for building His church to fade into the background. We have relegated His mission to the lost to some kind of optional church program, and we've paid a very dear and eternal price. The good news is, we can change that. We can start reversing that today—and doing it is simpler and exponentially more effective than any big evangelism program you have ever tried. In fact, oikos is both the most efficient evangelism process and the most effective discipleship process you've probably never heard of!

"If you try to reach everyone, you'll reach no one."

CHAPTER 4
FOCUSED ON FOCUS

What is the purpose of your church? Do you even know? When I ask people to tell me what the purpose of their church is, most of them try to recall a verse or tell me about some noble endeavor. But, more often than not, their responses don't have anything to do with the purpose of a church.

Executing a plan requires focus and a solid knowledge of our purpose. Purpose, planning and focus are intertwined so tightly they're essentially inseparable. When we understand our purpose clearly, then we can work our plan confidently with laser-like focus.

And while we're on the subject, you don't get to vote on the purpose for your church and neither do your leaders. Your opinion doesn't matter and neither do theirs. Don't be upset, I'm not being condescending because my opinion doesn't matter either. The purpose of the church was given to us by Jesus, the Head of the church. Our job is not to come up with it—our job is to execute it.

My mission in life is to help educate Christians about their reason for being alive—to help them discover their purpose, and then prepare them to be effective at fulfilling it. What we call evangelism is, in reality, only the first scene in a drama entitled "Worldchange." It would be a ridiculous waste of our created design, not to mention of the precious time we have on this planet, if we settle for anything less than pouring ourselves into the process of changing the world.

When the truth that God put us here for a reason—to be a part of the greatest initiative in world history—burrows deep roots into the soul of a believer, and they understand that no one else can fulfill that purpose in their relational world as well as they can, then something transformational happens. When we recognize that our church, your church, my church, the whole church, exists solely, and I mean solely, to prepare you and I to better fulfill that purpose, suddenly any local church becomes a much more compelling place to be. When people live in the everyday reality of doing life with their oikos, going to church becomes a "want to," not a "have to." It becomes more compelling, because the rest of the week depends on it!

THE GOD OF THE NICHE

I'm going to take a shot in the dark here—when the Christmas season rolls around again, I don't think you're going to give the same gift to everybody on your list. Actually, neither will I. Certain gifts are appropriate for some while other gifts are more appropriate for others. Well, God approaches gifting the same way—neither does He give everybody in His family the same spiritual gifts or everybody in your church the same spiritual gifts. When Jesus designed His church, He niched it for maximum performance. He gave each of us certain very specific spiritual abilities.

In fact, if a group of us were together in a big room right now, (I actually do this when I speak on this subject) I'd have everybody in the room raise their right hand and take the spiritual gifts vow. "Please repeat after me, 'I stink *(I stink)* at most everything *(at most everything)*.' Put your hands down. You passed."

When you think about it, none of us are very good at very much! God has created us all to be clumsy at most everything. The reason He designed us that way—to be so inept at so many things—is because He wants us to focus on only a few things. He wants us to become specialists. He wants us to become very good at one thing or a very short list of some things.

Perhaps you've heard the phrase, "You've gotta find your niche." Well, what is a niche? By definition, a niche is a position or activity, that particularly suits somebody's talents and personality, or that somebody can make his or her own.

Believe it or not, that was precisely the strategy Jesus utilized in forming the church. One of the primary "gifts" passages is 1 Corinthians 12, where it says, "God has placed the parts in the body, every one of them, just as He wanted them to be." (verse 18)

When it comes to changing the world God has niched us again! He wants all of us to be involved, but with certain, very specific people. And if you feel that your job is to witness to everybody, then you probably aren't witnessing to anybody. Your job is not to witness to the whole world, just like your job is not to run the whole church or exercise every spiritual gift on the list. Your job is not even to necessarily look for somebody to witness to. Granted, we represent Christ to anyone we come into contact with, and some of the best times in life are those spontaneous moments when we make a spiritual difference in the life of somebody we hadn't known before. But for most of us, those moments are rare, and for good reason. Our primary responsibility is simply to be prepared to minister the grace of

God to those groups of people He has already directed us to. It's simple and it's efficient!

At HDC our purpose is clearly stated, "To prepare every generation to change their worlds for Christ." Notice that *their* worlds are not *the* world. "Niche thyself."

Guy Kawasaki is one of the original evangelists for MacIntosh Computers. In an interview with Willow Creek's Magazine he discussed the topic of innovation in ministry. "If you want to be effective," he said, "then you have to niche thyself. If you try to reach everyone, you'll reach no one." [1] That's true in the business environment in the Silicon Valley, and it's also true in the church.

LASER LIGHT FOCUS

Jesus told us we are the light of the world, so let's consider light for a moment—and not just any light, but light in its most effective and powerful form—laser light. Light-Amplification-by-Stimulated-Emission-of-Radiation. A laser is a device that creates and amplifies a narrow intense beam of what physicists call coherent light.

I'm certainly not a scientist, but here's the deal. Atoms emit radiation. Normally they radiate their light in random directions at random times and that's called *incoherent* light.

That is a technical term for what we would consider to be an unorganized jumble of photons going in all different directions. Incoherent light is what we call soft light, allowing people to enjoy the ambiance of a social setting.

The trick in generating *coherent* light, a single or just a few frequencies going in one precise direction, is to find the right atoms with the right internal storage mechanisms and create an environment in which they can all cooperate—so that they all give up their light precisely at the right time and in the right direction. When you can do that, the result is pretty impressive. Coherent light is not soft light, it's flat-out powerful light, allowing people to accomplish things they've never been able to do before.

The power of focused light is seemingly endless in virtually every element of our lives. It has added a new dimension of efficiency in medicine, in weaponry, in electronic entertainment devices, in construction—you name it. And don't forget the church. I've been in way too many soft churches, where personal comfort trumps mission—but the truth is, I want to lead a powerful one. The difference between Christians who are coherent and Christians who are incoherent is this element of laser sharp focus. Everything and everyone cannot be a priority to us—or nothing and no one will be. Every caring believer wants the world to know Jesus, but if we try to evangelize everyone we will end up evangelizing no one.

STAY HOME

There's nothing quite like watching five-year-olds play basketball. Or baseball. Or soccer. I'm pretty sure that's not an exhaustive list, but it's the extent of my personal observations. As a grandfather now, I am blessed to be able to enjoy a second run with youth sports leagues—and I'm happy to report that not much has changed in the last twenty years. Let me describe each scene.

A five-year-old basketball game: twelve kids chasing a basketball.

A five-year-old baseball game: twenty kids chasing a baseball.

A five-year-old soccer game: ten kids chasing a soccer ball.

As a youth basketball league coach, my greatest challenge has always been to instill discipline—but at that age we're not talking about a workout regimen, we're talking about remembering your place on the field or the court. "Listen kids, I promise you in advance that Coach Tom will never be mad at you. When I'm yelling, it's only because I want you to hear me above all the other noises in a very loud gymnasium." And what did they hear me yell more than anything? "Stay home." Which being interpreted means, remember your area on the floor!

At that age, we exclusively played a zone defense. I used a smothering full-court trap for about a month, but the other coaches reminded me that shutouts in a five-year old basketball league were not good for kids' esteem. But with a half-court zone defense, each player has a particular area to cover, depending on where the ball happens to be on the court at any particular point in time.

In his first year of tee-ball, our grandson happened to be the fastest kid on the team. For the first few months, wherever the ball was hit, he was always the first to arrive. If he was playing third base and the ball was hit over the first-baseman's head, he was the first of twenty players to arrive in right field. He'd jump on the ball and the other nineteen kids would pile on top of him. Toward the end of that rookie season the kids finally started to understand good gamesmanship—stay home!

No matter what position you play or how athletic you might be, worldchange is a team sport. Support your teammates, to be sure, but the bottom line is to learn your position and stay home!

GOOD SOIL

A high-profile pastor was recently teaching the parable of the sower—he identified the four soils as an indication that most seed would never take root. His conclusion—since only 25% of the seed finds its mark, make sure you spread an awful lot of seed! By the way, I have the utmost respect for said pastor, but when you have a mega-budget, it's a little easier to read a shotgun approach to ministry into the text. But I don't work with a mega-budget—HDC happens to be a mega-church without a mega-budget, so we bring a long-barrel approach to the discussion.

Because I see everything, including the Scriptures, through an oikos lens anyway, my takeaway from the parable of the sower happens to be a bit different. I suppose you could contrast the amount of seed that found its mark to the total amount of seed that was sown—which would be 25%. Or, you could focus on how much of the seed that landed on the good soil found its mark—which happens to be 100%! My conclusion—efficiency requires that you identify where the good soil happens to be *before* you plant and then scatter your seed there.

"Other seed fell on good soil, where it produced a crop—a hundred, sixty or thirty times what was sown." (Matthew 13:8)

So let's focus on the right soil, the eight to fifteen people God has strategically and supernaturally placed in our world. Let's get focused on focus.

PART 2:

CLARIFYING YOUR PURPOSE

"Good is the enemy of great."

CHAPTER 5
BREAKING NEWS

Have you noticed how enamored broadcast news outlets can be with the term, "Breaking News?" You turn on a news channel, they play their theme music and pretty soon, "Breaking News." Like every five minutes there's somehow "Breaking News." You know, "Breaking News...Democrats protest the Republican proposal!" That's not even news! Even the commercials are being written as though they were "Breaking News." But because the media tries to make everything important to us, nothing seems all that important. It's the same principle as with the boy who cried "Wolf!"—elevating the less important always diminishes the more important.

Some years ago, I read an article about a guy who went to a church conference, much like many of the ones I've participated in. During the three days of the conference, he heard this line, "The most important thing you can do for your church is…" and then the presenter offered his featured something. He heard it so often that he began writing down every occasion someone said it. At the end of the event, he realized that he heard that line 26 times in three days!

We have to know that there can't be 26 most important things for you to do at your church! There is only one *most* important thing that any church does. And, by definition, everything else has to be less important. That doesn't mean they're unimportant, it means they're less important.

I've always believed that most churches are like most Christians, they try to do too much. And, in doing so, the most important thing gets lost in the shuffle. Jim Collins is one of our generation's most respected business analysts. He put it as succinctly as anyone could—"Good is the enemy of great." [1]

There are plenty of "good" things we could be about. But are those things squeezing out our chance to do something extraordinary? Could our success actually be just another form of failure because we've abandoned what our priority should be?

Jesus has called us to change the world. So how are you going to fit that into your schedule today? Pastors are notorious for expecting a ton of admittedly good things out of a congregation. But if we're not careful, churchgoers will be so consumed with churchgoing, committees, boards and all of the projects we "need" their help with, they will lose whatever passion they could muster to do the thing that matters most! And we would have no one to blame but ourselves. People simply do not have enough emotional energy to be passionate about very much.

ANYTHING LESS THAN EVERYTHING IS A PROGRAM

Oikos is not a program that we do at our church. In fact, at HDC oikos is not just everything, it is the only thing! And if anyone recommends a system or programming proposal that does not line up with the purpose of the church—preparing (individuals in) every generation to change their (relational) worlds for Christ," the conversation doesn't last very long. It's not that we don't have systems and programs because we do—but only if they feed into our core purpose of equipping people to contribute to worldchange by reaching their oikos more effectively.

You and I might live on the same planet but we don't share the same world, because I won't even meet most of the people in yours. But that's actually very freeing to me—I'm thankful that God let me off the hook with your world. He knew I wouldn't have time for two worlds. I'm free to deal with mine, the specific group that God has given me to target.

TARGET ACQUIRED

To a submariner there are two kinds of vessels in the water, submarines and targets. As followers of Christ, we face a similar scenario. Here's another way to look at your oikos.

Just for a moment, suppose you had the capacity to declare to everyone on the planet that you were a faithful follower of Jesus Christ—that we had the global communications department of some worldwide agency hook you up to speak to everyone in the entire world, translating your words into every language on earth and that all seven or eight billion people heard you boldly declare that you were a faithful follower of Jesus Christ. You know what? Only around eight to fifteen people out of the entire global population would know if you were really telling the truth. That is your oikos! They are your target! They are where our primary focus should be, both as individuals and as a corporate church.

We could also look at your oikos as your purpose in life because that group of people actually frames the primary reason you woke up this morning. There are many ideas floating out there regarding the purpose of church or even the purpose of a Christian life. I grew up in a ministry family, so I've probably heard them all.

THE GOSPEL OF SIN MANAGEMENT

For a lot of us, the primary purpose of the church seemed to be all about ensuring that Christians became more and more obedient to the Scriptures. Early on, that's the one that stuck with me—I thought we attended church so that we could talk about ways to sin less during the coming week than we had during the last. Dallas Willard talks about the Christian life being relegated to what he calls, "the gospel of sin management." [2] And while sin management, as he describes it, is important, it's not an end to itself. It is simply a means to a greater end.

I see it as something like a sports contract for a professional athlete. Some of the most successful and highly paid athletes in the world are not allowed to participate in certain activities that are considered dangerous by the management of a particular sports franchise. They are forbidden to do some things because those things would pose a risk to their contractual purpose.

For example, some players' contracts don't allow them to go skydiving or motocross racing. They might not be allowed to engage in snow skiing or water sports because they're just too risky. But those athletes are not paid incredible salaries to ensure that they will *not* do those things. They are paid that money so they will perform on the field or on the court—to throw shutouts and touchdown passes and make three-pointers. But in order to make sure those guys can "do the do's," they are under contract to make sure they "don't do the don'ts."

That's how the don'ts should operate in the Christian life. We cannot define the "Thou shalt nots" as the purpose for our lives. Being obedient just enhances our potential to do what we're actually under contract for. You do realize that we too are under contract, don't you? The Bible says that we are not our own either, that our contracts have been "bought at a price." (1 Corinthians 6:19-20) We are now under obligation to fulfill the call of the One who purchased us, who redeemed us with His blood.

Earlier I said that most young people don't go to church because they haven't been given a good enough reason and, I can tell you from experience, the prospect of sin management is certainly not a compelling reason to attend. In fact, it has never been a compelling reason to attend church. When you were a kid you didn't want to go to church just to make sure you didn't mess up, and neither did I. Besides, no matter how well we manage sin, we will never manage it well enough to deserve Heaven.

"It is by grace you have been saved, through faith—and this is not from yourselves, it is the gift of God—not by works, so that no one can boast." (Ephesians 2:8-9)

According to my position in Christ I became sinless at the age of seven, the moment I received Him into my life, when "in him I became the righteousness of God!" (2 Corinthians 5:21) But when it comes to my "practice," it's a whole different story. The way I see it, I won't be completely sin free in practice until the microsecond after I croak. Only then will I become absolutely holy in every single respect. At that moment, I'll be with Him and there won't be any more sin in my life *to* manage. Between the day I gave my heart to Christ in 1962 and that amazing day I enter His presence, there must be something incredibly important for me to do that includes more than not sinning.

Our challenge is to find that something and to make it the main thing in our lives because our purpose, destiny and ultimately our eternal rewards are all wrapped up in it.

"Good intentions are no excuse for incompetence."

CHAPTER 6
THE MAIN THING

The main thing in life is to keep the main thing the main thing. That's a constant theme at HDC, but it takes work to keep number one number one, as other important aspects of the Christian life keep trying to push their way up the list. But even mission critical elements do not deserve *main* thing status. Rick Warren challenged us to keep our focus in this life on what we won't be able to do in the next—"God's kept us here on Earth to fulfill a purpose we cannot do better in Heaven."[1] We will always tend to stray away from our life mission when we make even important things too "main thing."

Everything we will mention in this chapter frames a significant component to spiritual growth and discipleship, preparing us for our all-important role as worldchangers. But, keep in mind, the church only has one real purpose and Jesus was clear on what that was—"to seek and to save the lost." So, while we enthusiastically engage each of the following components to our personal growth, we must be careful to always keep the main thing the main thing! As Peter Drucker said, "Good intentions are no excuse for incompetence." [2]

CORPORATE WORSHIP

Some people look at the purpose of the church as being wrapped up in corporate worship. All of the worship leaders at HDC know I love to worship. They know I appreciate all they do in bringing our communities and campuses to the throne of God every weekend. But with all due respect to the worship leaders out there, the best worship in the Universe is not in any local church. The best worship in the Universe isn't even *in* the Universe—it's around the throne of God. If corporate worship is the purpose of the church, God might as well take us home to Heaven right now so we can get on with it! Besides, in our carnality, we'll never be able to worship down here the way we should.

"The Lord says: 'These people come near to me with their mouth and honor me with their lips, but their hearts are far from me. Their worship of me is based on merely human rules they have been taught.' " (Isaiah 29:13)

When you walk into a worship service, even if you're about to hear the world's greatest worship band, preparing to sing with one of the premier worship leaders in the country or are walking into the greatest worship event in the history of the church—you would still walk into that auditorium distracted by all the other things that are going on around you. On the way to the event, you may have had an argument with your spouse—which for some has become a Christian tradition!

My point is, often we walk into church and we're frustrated about what happened before church or concerned about what's going to happen after church. You can be frustrated about the deal that didn't go down the week before; about the issue you're going to have to resolve on Monday morning; about the fact that the nursery workers didn't show up when they were supposed to and, by the time you got into the auditorium, someone had snagged your regular seat—and now you're really ticked off!

Then when you get into your seat things get worse—you notice the guy leading worship is just a little off key; or the music's a little loud; or maybe the guy in the choir, front-row, second from the left, has a really bizarre comb-over. You can't even worship without all of those things working against you. And the purpose of the church is supposed to be corporate worship? It can't be. The purpose of the church can't be something that is better accomplished after the church doesn't exist anymore.

FELLOWSHIP

I've been in a few fellowship churches. You know the type, where the biggest thing on the calendar is the next potluck fellowship. It's all about getting from one social event to the next. Electing officers. Lots of committees.

"Let's get this service over with so we can all get to the Fellowship Hall!" Or, "We can't start a second worship service—if we do, we'll divide the congregation." Or, "We don't like the fact that the church has gotten so big—we don't know everybody's name anymore!"

Now don't get me wrong, there's certainly nothing wrong with fellowship. I enjoy good fellowship as much as the next guy. It just can't be the purpose of the church—because the best fellowship in any universe is in the same place you'll find the best worship! So if fellowship is what the church is all about, we might as well hope God punches our ticket sooner than later.

BIBLE KNOWLEDGE

At this point, you may be tempted to push back with, "What about discipleship?" Actually, it's one of the primary concerns that people initially express about an oikocentric ministry model. But my question simply is, "What is the goal of your discipleship efforts?"

I grew up learning the Bible under the ministry of some of the most capable pastors and teachers in America. Now I love helping people grow in their knowledge about God's Word. But the Bible itself says that enhancing biblical knowledge for its own sake is dangerous—in the Apostle Paul's words, it "puffs up." (1 Corinthians 8:1)

After explaining oikos in a recent phone conversation, a pastor asked me, "What do you do for the mature Christians?" I said, "We don't have any" (extended awkward silence). "We don't have any mature Christians, but we do have 12,000 *maturing* Christians!"

A typical model for local church ministry reflects two strategies for two distinct classifications of Christians— the mature and the immature. Whereas the New Testament describes the goal of the Christian experience as becoming "mature," it also reminds us that we will never actually reach that ideal this side of eternity. So HDC has dropped the traditional mindset of the "haves and the have nots," the mature and the immature, and focuses instead on the goal that we all share—that of a maturing believer. Certainly, some leadership elements should not be available to a Christian novice. On the other hand, I'm not sure that developing fully devoted followers of Christ is even possible in this life. And our determination to relationally separate new believers from their pagan pasts and acculturate them into our "fellowships" can actually sabotage a local church ministry by short-circuiting the organic process of worldchange.

The traditional paradigm for discipleship requires an extended season of formal training that presumes to better prepare Christians to begin their active role in evangelism. But after the required regimen is completed, usually lasting months, if not years, "mature" believers have not only wasted their best season of oikocentric potential but, more often than not, find themselves now disconnected from the group they would have most likely reached.

Dr. Walt White, a missiologist in Bangladesh, reflects a similar concern overseas. "Many of us feel that we have failed to take the principle of the oikos seriously. We have somehow usually applied a different process for evangelism and the establishment of the church among tribal societies than we have among those from the major historic religions. Our individualistic Western thinking led us to a style of evangelism termed 'extractionist.' That is, it disregarded the inquirer's oikos and even viewed it as a barrier rather than a gift from God! So, we ripped a new believer from their oikos, often doing so even before the person had come to faith in Jesus or certainly before they had the opportunity to come to any degree of maturity. Then we wondered why they were unable to reach their oikos with the Good News. One obvious reason was that it sounded like horrible news to the believer's birth oikos, not good news. So, we then had to provide him/her with a new oikos, almost always made up entirely of people who were already Christians. If there were non-Christians still in their new oikos, those non-Christians had to ask themselves why they should trust this new believer when their birth oikos does not! And we wondered why it seemed they could reach almost no one, no matter how profound their salvation experience." [3]

Actually, most churches would not have to change many of the functional elements of discipleship systems that are already in place. They would simply need to readdress the purpose for any discipleship process, redefine the endgame. I mean, if believers are not being discipled to actually be disciples, then what's the point? By definition, you can't be a follower of Jesus Christ unless you are actually following Jesus Christ.

He who thinketh he leadeth but has no one following is only taking a walk! That quip might characterize some of us, but it certainly never characterized Jesus—He was often on the move but He was never just taking a walk. Jesus was on a mission—organizing and discipling His guys so that they could be fishers of men. Not that there was anything wrong with fishing for fish—it's just not what He came to do.

AFTER I DIE

The second after I die, I will enjoy better worship, have better fellowship and possess more knowledge about God than I ever will in this life. The same is true for you—but God has kept you here for the time being because he wants you to do something you cannot do in Heaven.

I may not be the sharpest tack on the board, but I'm thinking that if the purpose of the church is in any of the things we've discussed to this point, then I might not have a good reason to stick around. If anything other than an all-out effort "to seek and to save the lost" is the true purpose of the church, then the plan might as well be to just pray to receive Christ and then go on to Glory.

So here we are again. There truly are only two things you can do here that you can't do in Heaven—one is sin and the other is to share Christ with non-believers. Those are the two things that won't be present in Heaven—sin and non-believers. Which begs the question, which of those two things do you think God wants you to do while you're still here?

Once again, that is not to say the other things we've discussed are not important. Those other elements—worship, fellowship and discipleship are all vital to a believer's growth and the life of a local church. They all make us better prepared for our mission and allow us to more effectively fulfill the one and only purpose for our deployment here—to communicate God's grace to a world that desperately needs it. At HDC we call that keeping the main thing the main thing. But as a Star Trek geek, I know it by another term—The Prime Directive. And it seems that Christ followers have one of those as well!

"A Starship Captain's most solemn oath is that he will give his life, even his entire crew, rather than violate the Prime Directive." [1]

CHAPTER 7
THE PRIME DIRECTIVE

The Starship Enterprise was given a mission—to pioneer the exploration of deep space, "to boldly go where no man has gone before!" Kirk, Spock and rest of the crew were commissioned to seek out new life and new civilizations and bring the information they discovered on their voyages back to Starfleet. However, there was a Prime Directive—a cardinal rule, if you will. Under no circumstances were they to interfere with the development of any civilization.

The church also has a mission. Our challenge is not to go

where no one has ever gone, but to follow Jesus where He has already gone—into *this* world, and follow according to His directives. Unlike the Enterprise, we are not tasked with reaching other worlds, but to reach our own; and we are not looking to bring information back, but to deliver the information we've been entrusted with, to take the good news of Jesus to our worlds.

However, we too have a Prime Directive. Whereas the crew of the Enterprise was commanded never to interfere, as Captain Kirk warned, even if it meant the sacrifice of the entire crew, we are directed by the Head of the church to do exactly the opposite, to deliberately engage our world. The objective is not to leave our world unchanged, but to initiate a dramatic transformation of change. Anything less would be a waste of our photon torpedoes.

But, in all honesty, how realistic is it for any one of us to think that we could change the entire world, even if we worked at it full time? Not very. It wouldn't be fair to expect any of us to affect that level of change. So how can we fulfill the Greatest Commission ever, to go into the entire world with the good news of God's provision for the restoration of humanity?

Well, let's remember something about the day Jesus spoke those familiar words we call the Great Commission. He was speaking to *all* the disciples. He expected each of them to take a portion of the challenge but not for any of them to take on the whole thing. That approach never changed. Realistically, none of us could be given the responsibility for changing the whole world. But each one of us does have our own world, a much smaller world that we can dramatically and effectively impact. Those are the worlds that bear our unique signatures. Those are the worlds we will indeed change through a disciplined demonstration of godly character and timely words of perspective.

WHY WORLDCHANGE?

"Wait a minute, Tom, aren't we just talking about witnessing here?" Witnessing, yes. But "just," no! Here's the critical point—we must think beyond the required process and focus on the desired outcome. If you define a challenge simply in terms of the tasks involved, where's the motivation? It's become a simple (but not necessarily easy) "to do" list. Like we need another one of those!

For example, building a house can be an exhausting process. For an entire year you have to manage the individual tasks required (grading, concrete, framing, plumbing, electrical, painting, etc.). But rather than focusing on those tasks, new homeowners maintain their sanity by keeping the *outcome* in mind, how beautiful the finished product will be. Think about worldchange that way. Focusing on the individual tasks can wear you out before you even begin. So focus instead on the desired outcome—the transformation of people's lives and the birth of a new spiritual legacy. Reconciled marriages, renewed families, destructive addictions conquered—understanding outcome provides a category switch for the tasks involved—from "taxing" to "exhilarating," from "forced" to "natural."

The oikos model of evangelism is authentic, organic worldchange—one person's world at a time. This is so critical that it has framed the mission of our entire church and even defined the reason for HDC's placement in the high desert. Our mission statement declares that we exist solely "to prepare every generation to change their worlds for Christ."

A FUNNEL, NOT A BUCKET

The plan of redemption began with Israel. They were designated as the "Chosen People." The question is, what were they chosen for?

God made His commitment to humanity clear way back in the Old Testament. He was going to bring men and women from every nation back into a vital loving relationship with Himself. He chose a select group of people to be the vessels through whom He would fulfill that divine mission. Actually, when God launched that initiative they weren't even a group yet, they were just a guy. I guess you could say, Abraham was the Chosen Guy! And God told him:

"I will make you into a great nation and I will bless you; I will make your name great, and you will be a blessing. I will bless those who bless you, and whoever curses you I will curse; and all peoples on earth will be blessed through you." (Genesis 12:2-3) To make sure it was clear, the Abrahamic Covenant is repeated in Genesis 18:18; chapter 22:15, 18; chapter 26:4 and chapter 28:14.

But the Covenant was both a promise and a challenge. In time, Israel would become that nation, but they were chosen to be a funnel for God's blessing, not a bucket.

We see the literal fulfillment of that purpose in many Old Testament stories. For example, in Genesis 49:22, Jacob calls his son Joseph "... a fruitful vine, a fruitful vine near a spring, whose branches climb over a wall."

The story of Joseph details how one of those Chosen People fulfilled the Jewish mandate—by crossing his cultural lines and blessing the Gentile world with the love of God. That purpose has not changed. God still wants to accomplish what He began when He instituted the plan of redemption—reaching the entire world. He never intended that Israel would become grace collectors, but be grace channels. But when God blesses you, the "bucket mentality" is a hard one to resist. As a result, Israel tended to focus too much on the promise that was involved and began neglecting the challenge that was required.

For a while, that bucket mentality continued on into the formation of the church. The same resistance to outreach that had plagued the Jews before Jesus came continued to plague the Jews who recognized He was the Christ. Many of them only wanted to reach out to their own ethnic group. However, in Acts 15, at the Jerusalem Council, the church leaders finally realized God meant what He said from the beginning—that He was committed to going global with this thing and that whoever didn't get on board would be left behind!

"Therefore go and make disciples of all nations..." (Matthew 28:19)

"You will be my witnesses in Jerusalem, and in all Judea and Samaria, and to the ends of the earth." (Acts 1:8)

James concluded as he addressed the Council: "It is my judgment, therefore, that we should not make it difficult for the Gentiles who are turning to God." (Acts 15:19) Do we get that? That the call of the church is to connect the world with the good news of God's love? Thousands of years after the Bible was written, our job is not much different than the one God gave Abraham only twelve chapters in!

But are we ready for that? Or do our own churches suffer from that same bucket mentality? Does yours? Does our disinterest in the state of hopelessness of those all around us make it difficult for our neighbors and friends to see Jesus when they look at us? Jesus came "to seek and to save the lost." (Luke 19:10) Every day, when we roll out of the sack, that should matter. This is now *our* job. All of our job!

THE BIG PICTURE

The world's 5.3 billion people are divided into appoximately 24,000 people groups. Of those 24,000 groups, 12,000 are "reached." These comprise cultures where a viable indigenous church movement has been established.

On the other hand, 12,000 people groups, comprising 2.2 billion individuals, do not yet have a viable Christian representation. These groups include 4,000 Muslim people groups, 3,000 Tribal people groups, 2,000 Hindu people groups, 1,000 Chinese people groups, 1,000 Buddhist people groups and 1,000 other people groups, all with virtually no Evangelical Christian presence.

Understanding the specific task of the individual believer is the critical theme of this book. But understanding how that task fits into that big picture of God's plan for a global Christian movement is also important. As we will see next, changing the world is a process that involves three distinct steps, and God has a different method of revealing Himself with each one.

"It's like Deja Vu all over again!"

Chapter 8
BUILDING BRIDGES

Have you ever seen someone you think you recognize, you just don't know why or from what context? Like Yogi Berra said, sometimes "It's like Deja Vu all over again!" As missiologists explore unreached cultures, it becomes more and more apparent that God had arrived long before the missionaries did. Legends, oral traditions and written cultural histories tend to reveal different expressions of the same biblical principles embedded within different cultures all over the world. That's why, whenever a pioneering believer enters an unreached culture and shares the

Gospel, they often hear, "Wait a minute, we know this Man, Jesus!" Or, "We already understand about sin or grace." And they're right! God laid the groundwork well in advance of the missionaries' arrival. When they eventually show up, it becomes a task of connecting those more ambiguous ancient cultural representations of truth with the clear message of the Gospel.

Solomon said it very eloquently. "(God) has made everything beautiful in its time. He has also set eternity in the human heart." (Ecclesiastes 3:11)

Paul was intrigued by the fact that Gentiles seemed to behave as if they were consciously conforming to the Law of Moses, even though they had never heard of it. He later came to conclude:

"When Gentiles, who do not have the law, do by nature things required by the law, they are a law for themselves, even though they do not have the law. They show that the requirements of the law are written on their hearts, their consciences also bearing witness, and their thoughts sometimes accusing, and at other times even defending them." (Romans 2:14-15)

THE LESSON OF THE ATHENIANS

One of history's most powerful expressions of God's bridge building nature begins with a pandemic crisis in the early history of Athens. As the story begins, the situation was critical—thousands of Athenians had already died. A plague had descended on that great city and her people were quickly losing hope. They had prayed and sacrificed to every god they knew, but none had responded. The members of the great Athenian Council were desperate; so much so, they were willing to ask anyone, even foreigners, for advice. After much debate, they agreed on a plan. Within days, an emissary was dispatched to the Island of Crete to find a man named Epimenides, a renowned philosopher, on whose wise shoulders the fate of that great city would rest.

Epimenides walked the streets of Athens, appraising the dire situation he was finally able to see first hand. He concluded that the Athenian people must have somehow offended a god they did not know existed. That god, therefore, had not yet heard their appeal for mercy. Epimenides then requested access to a large flock of sheep. He released them all early the next morning to graze. He and his aids watched closely to see if any of the sheep would lie down.

What sheep tended not to do, he believed, was rest early in the morning when they are notoriously hungry. Therefore, if any did, his logic concluded, this unknown god would be identifying which sheep he would accept as a sacrifice in lieu of his wrath. To the Athenians' surprise, several sheep actually did lie down to rest, and each one of them was slaughtered on the very spots they had rested, sacrificed on altars that were quickly built to honor this unknown god. Within days, the plague lifted.

The events I just described are not simply embedded in Greek mythology, they are part of recorded history. In fact, 800 years later, at least some of those altars were still in place. Diogenes Laertius, a third century Greek author, confirms, "Altars may be found in different parts of Attica with no name inscribed upon them, which are memorials of this atonement." [1]

Sandwiched in history between those two men is someone you're probably more familiar with. More than 500 years after Epimenides and 300 years before Laertius, the Apostle Paul found something on Athens' Mars Hill that would provide him an opportunity to explain a different kind of sacrifice to the Athenians. A student of history and well acquainted with Epimenides, Paul boldly declared, "Men of Athens! I see that in every way you are very religious. For as I walked around and looked carefully at your objects of worship, I even found an altar with this inscription: TO AN UNKNOWN GOD. So you are ignorant of the very thing you worship—and this is what I am going to proclaim to you." (Acts 17:22-23)

God had planted, deep in their history, an explanation of who He was and then He prepared Paul to help the Greeks make the connection. On that day, Athens would learn about another Lamb whose sacrifice would appease God's wrath and save the world.

THE BRIDGE BUILDER

God had essentially set up the Greek people to understand the Gospel—and it seems they are not alone. According to Don Richardson, whether you talk about the Jewish sacrificial system, the Dyak Tribe of Borneo or the Asmats of New Guinea, the same phenomenon exists. "Before the Gospel arrives, no matter the indigenous culture or religion of a people group, God has already designed a prolific feature of that culture to serve as a bridge to the person and work of Jesus." [1]

God has made His own introduction to unreached people groups. So by the time believers show up in an unreached culture the emphasis is less about an introduction and more about an explanation.

One of the women from our church traveled with a missionary organization to China for a short-term mission trip. When she returned she told us their story. "We were sharing the story of Noah's Ark and how God's grace had saved all eight people of Noah's family. 'We know about that story,' they said. 'How do you know about Noah?' we asked. 'Well, we didn't know his name until you told us, but in our language the Chinese character for grace is eight people in a boat.' We were blown away! He was not only with us on that trip, He had gone ahead of us."

"All authority in heaven and on earth has been given to me. Therefore go and make disciples of all nations, baptizing them in the name of the Father and of the Son and of the Holy Spirit, and teaching them to obey everything I have commanded you. And surely I am with you always, to the very end of the age." (Matthew 28:18-20)

USED BY GOD

So then, how does God use a reached culture, such as ours, to evangelize an unreached culture? Once God has *introduced* Himself, He *explains* Himself through the corporate efforts of the established church as they reach out to a new culture. To efficiently function in that capacity, the established church needs to develop a widescreen vision, the ability to see the immediate, local evangelistic opportunities (found in their worlds) as well as the global evangelistic opportunities (in the world).

Acts 13:2-3 records that, "While they were worshiping the Lord and fasting, the Holy Spirit said, 'Set apart for me Barnabas and Saul for the work to which I have called them.' So after they had fasted and prayed, they placed their hands on them and sent them off."

A FULL-COURT PRESS
GOD'S PLAN FOR GLOBAL EVANGELISM

EVANGELISTIC ARENA	DIVINE ACTION	PROCESS USED
TO UNREACHED CULTURES	GOD INTRODUCES HIMSELF	THROUGH CULTURAL IMPRINT
THROUGH A REACHED CULTURE	GOD EXPLAINS HIMSELF	THROUGH GLOBAL MISSIONS EFFORTS
WITHIN A REACHED CULTURE	GOD REVEALS HIMSELF	THROUGH OIKOS NETWORKS

This book is dedicated to the demonstration of God's grace within a reached culture. But whether you're an ambassador of the Gospel traveling to an unreached culture on the other side of the world, or simply walking across the street to help a friend in your world, you will eventually find a bridge that He has supernaturally and strategically placed for you to cross. It might be a mutual friend or a common experience. It could be a love for fishing or cooking or Shakespeare; gas for a lawn mower or a television set that quits working ten minutes before the biggest game of the year. It may loom as obvious as the Golden Gate or be so subtle you won't realize it was there until after you've crossed it. But God is always the engineer, every relationship's architect.

We should never storm into our relational worlds, boldly declaring that we have arrived to save their sorry selves. We were never designed to wear arrogance very well, but we must never be shy about our mission either. Every time we open a dialogue or pull up to Starbucks for coffee or try to figure out a way to invite someone to an Easter service, we should do so with confidence and anticipation.

Eventually, we will stumble across one of those bridges, one that God has built at some point in their past. And on the other side of that bridge you'll find that same God, already waiting. He'll be sitting right there next to that member of your oikos who, without even knowing it, has always been destined to finally hear about that unknown God and His unbelievable love.

"All I had to do was keep turning left."

CHAPTER 9
STOVETOP MANAGEMENT

Anyone who knows me knows that I'm a simple man. The simpler the idea, the more it resonates with me. In that sense, I guess I'm like George Robson. When asked how he won the Indy 500, the Canadian driver simply replied, "All I had to do was keep turning left."[1] My gift as a teacher seems to be in breaking down an idea into its most fundamental form, or as some have said, "to put the cookies on the bottom shelf." Maybe that's why I'm so drawn to the Bible—most of it is self-explanatory. When someone tells me that they don't read the Bible because they can't understand it, I know they gave up pretty quickly. "Just keep reading," I tell them, "It will explain itself."

Certainly, the Bible contains some concepts too lofty for any of us to even pretend to fully understand (the price we pay for mortality), but those passages comprise only a small fraction of the Scriptures. Other sections have layers of truth that only those who take their study seriously will ever appreciate. But even the simplest among us would be able to understand most passages if, like George, we just 'keep turning (those pages) left!" Had God wanted to remain a mystery, He wouldn't have written the Bible at all. He wants us all to understand it, He just doesn't want us to think we can improve it. He knows that if we try to make it better, we'll only make it more complicated— and the simple truth it contains will be lost in an intricate web of competing theologies. It's hard to hear the still small voice of the Gospel over the angry shouts of a factious church.

The most impressive thing about Dr. Arn's presentation was how humble it was! Don't get me wrong, it was incredibly impactful—but it was also just so incredibly simple. Jesus' plan to build His church had never needed modification. From generation to generation, from culture to culture, from Testament to Testament, it was as uncomplicated as it was consistent.

Until that day I had hated the thought of witnessing. The funny thing was, up to that day, God hated the way I thought about it too! Hearing Dr. Arn sent me on a journey I have yet to complete. What he said stirred me to action. I investigated it and it was true. I tried it and it worked! I taught it and it changed the way people saw their world. Now I lead a church full of people who are energized by it, and I am reminded everyday that it really is that impactful, that it really is that simple—and that the world really is that small.

A UNIFIED CHURCH

One of the most exciting things about the oikos model of ministry is how effectively it can unify a church. Now that you've considered why your church exists, ask yourself if that purpose is a supportive fit for your life purpose?

Oikos provides that support—or as we said earlier, oikos fits! The purpose of the Christian life and role of the church *should* be a natural fit. If the purpose of a believer's life is to both clearly display God's grace within their oikos and to explain their faith as conversations develop—then it follows that preparing believers to fulfill those objectives is the reason for any church's existence. Unfortunately, some churches have so many programs the people can't possibly stay on task.

I believe the number one reason that leadership teams and church families have conflict is because we so easily lose sight of our mission. If I have time to be critical of you, then I evidently have too much time on my hands! I need to get busy and refocus on the reason God put me here.

I'm drawn to the passage in 1 Corinthians 1:12, where Paul describes division in the fellowship: "I'm of Paul," "I'm of Apollos," "I'm of Cephas," and then all the real spiritual guys say, "I'm of Jesus." The Apostle identifies the conflict in the Corinthian church and then says, a few verses later, in effect, "You better knock off the infighting or the cross of Christ will be emptied of its power." (verse 17)

Stop and think about that possibility—that something is so strong it can suck the power right out of the cross! That's really something. And that something is division in a church. God can use a lot of different kinds of churches—different sizes, different styles, different doctrinal bents. He just doesn't seem to use a church where the people are fighting each other instead of the enemy. When I talk to leaders where there's this divided loyalty going on in their churches, all I can do is remind them of what Paul said—"You better clean that up or your mission is over." The power of the cross is, to a significant degree, vested in the unity of those who bear the message of the cross.

STOVETOP MANAGEMENT

So what do you do when God assembles a group of people from different religious and cultural backgrounds under one church roof? First, you recognize that they are there. In the membership process at HDC, I go through a little exercise.

"Okay," I say, "How many of you come from an Assembly of God background?" Hands go up. "Calvary Chapel?" Another group of hands go up. Through the list I go, "Methodist, Presbyterian, Church of Christ, Baptist? What about Catholic? Or how about a Mennonite or two?" It's quickly apparent to everyone, we've got 'em all!

Secondly, you must accept the probability that they will never be united on the basis of anyone's doctrinal views. In fact, the larger a church becomes and the more doctrinal passions are present, the greater potential there is for division. And that division will get ugly, I promise you—unless there is a compelling and even overwhelmingly greater purpose for that church to work together. I guess you could say, church families have to manage the stovetop—to be trained in what issues deserve *front burner* status and which issues must be relegated to the *back burner*.

Church leaders tend to dream out loud with comments like this—"I'm praying that our church experiences revival, even asking God for large numbers of people to come to Christ and then become an active part of our church!" When I hear things like that, my initial response is, "Really? Be careful what you ask for! Are you sure you want all of those diverse, opinionated, probably won't agree much, amateur theologs coming to your church?" If you do (and I believe you should), you better frame the debates that will take place in the years that follow *before* those people actually get there!

You know as well as I do, if you want to start a war in your church just go to any meeting and bring up one of the more controversial elements of your church's doctrinal statement—then sit back and watch people devour each other. They came in smiling, shaking hands and hugging everybody, drinking coffee, enjoying a donut, and then, boom! What happened? Stovetop mismanagement.

As a church separates into factions, divisions deepen, church meetings become unbearable and, all the while, none of us are one bit closer to changing our worlds for Christ. In fact, we'll probably be further away from any productivity after the meeting than we were before we came.

Let me be clear—theological orthodoxy is incredibly important to me. In a healthy church, one driven by the right purpose, even difficult discussions about controversial doctrines are not only possible, they're encouraged. But only because we can end virtually all of those discussions with, "Isn't it great that agreeing on this matter isn't essential to our real reason for coming together as a church?" I would never suggest that orthodox theology is not important. But since you'd be hard pressed to find two people who have exactly the same view of orthodoxy, I'm just suggesting that you give them something more important to do than argue about their opinions!

For the sake of this discussion, let's just say that we assembled representatives from every Christian denomination and sect in the world and, after a lengthy conversation, settled all of the arguments about every doctrinal question that any of us have ever had—and that we finally agree on everything. Further, let's say that everything we agreed on was actually correct. Obviously I'm dreaming here but, even if we could pull that off, we would have only accomplished what is going to be accomplished anyway about one second after the last one to leave walks through the Pearly Gates! So what's the purpose of life? Can simply vying for doctrinal purity really be the point of the church? I'm not saying that theological debate is unimportant, I'm just asking if it is really the purpose of the church. Or did God just give us what He gave us to provide essential truth, sufficient insight to accomplish our purpose and yet, at the same time, hold diverse views on most things with humility as we work together to build His Kingdom?

The same Paul who championed truth also made quite a case for differences of opinion on "disputable matters"—all because he understood the church's mission. He knew that, if the church were successful in her mission, then she would necessarily become increasingly diverse.

"I appeal to you, brothers and sisters, in the name of our Lord Jesus Christ, that all of you agree with one another in what you say and that there be no divisions among you, but that you may be perfectly united in mind and thought." (1 Corinthians 1:10) For many of us, that has historically meant, "Let's argue until we all agree." But maybe it actually means, "Let's stop arguing because it doesn't matter that we all agree on very much."

Believe me, I've got some pretty specific and unwavering views on most every topic, theological and otherwise. When I teach the Word, I speak with conviction and believe that I am correct about every issue. If challenged that I "think I'm right about everything," I always push back—"Of course I do! If I thought I was wrong about something, I'd change my mind so I could think I was right again!" But after all of the arguments are over about who's right and who's wrong, what are we doing to change the world? After all, isn't that the point?

One of the first things that people want to know about HDC is how large a church it is. A typical conversation goes something like this:

"How big is your church?'

"We have a little over 150,000 people."

(With an incredulous look) "My, goodness, you have 150,000 people in your church?"

"Yes, but 138,000 of them don't attend yet!"

Can you imagine how much more diverse HDC would be if they actually ever came? And yet it is for those 138,000 that the other 12,000 have been asked to live another day.

Like a ship with many different sails, if we don't all work in unity we can't accomplish anything. Not only that, even if we get all the sails set the same way but there is no wind, guess what? We still go nowhere. Just like a ship's sails have to be set properly and there must be a wind to give the ship steerage way, so too must a church have a common purpose among its people and its leadership, and the wind of the Holy Spirit to energize that one purpose!

JOB SECURITY

For people in my vocation, job security often means just keeping a church together. So how can we hope to do that when we have such diverse congregations? Up until now, you might have actually been proud to say, "My church is *not* diverse." Well, if that's the case, then you're not reaching out to your community because your community is very diverse. In fact, if people are coming into your church and they are finding Christ then your church is actually becoming more diverse all the time. And eventually it's going to catch up with you! How are you going to keep the group together? You have to keep them and yourself on mission. If you can, you simply won't have the time or energy to think about how wrong everybody else in the church might be about things that are clearly less important than the mission.

You see, oikos is the main thing because it contextualizes a purpose we all share. When believers figure that out, it becomes the great equalizer in any church. It doesn't matter how good looking you are or how unattractive you might be. It doesn't matter how tall you are or how short you are, if you have money or if you're flat broke. Your ethnic background? Theological background? Don't matter. Actually, what really matters is that you've got eight to fifteen people that God has supernaturally and strategically placed in your sphere of influence, and so do I. That means we've all got the same job to do today—to figure out ways to better communicate to them the amazing grace of God. When any group of believers catch that vision, they no longer have time to bicker and fight. Implemented effectively, oikocentricity creates a church full of partners, all pulling their own weight, all pulling their oars in the same direction.

HIGH HEAT

Keeping a group of people focused on a common purpose isn't easy. I mean, if Paul and Barnabas can't figure out how to work together, how are 12,000 non-apostles supposed to? By keeping the front burner fired up! Some of you reading this book have visited HDC and you know what that looks like. Every single week, in virtually every service, I'll say something to this effect, "God has brought eight to fifteen people into your sphere of influence. He has surrounded you with this group of individuals, strategically and supernaturally, because He wants to reach out to them and He wants to use you in the process." And then I'll continue, "And the Greeks called this group an...," and thousands of people will say in unison, "*oikos*," because they are never allowed to forget what the endgame looks like.

They're at our church because they're becoming better prepared to do the only thing that's worth waking up every day for. The laser sharp focus of this oikos strategy is what Jesus implemented from the very beginning. It has always been His main thing. And the main thing in life is to keep the main thing...

You can finish that line.

"If that's what you think, then that's all you'll ever be!"

CHAPTER 10
THAT'S THE SPIRIT!

Toward the end of his long and distinguished career in comedy, Milton Berle gave much of his time to performing for senior citizens at rest homes. "As long as I'm performing here, I'm not living here," he would say. One day, a resident sat through one of his performances somewhat aloof. Afterward, he approached her and asked her, "Excuse me ma'am, but do you know who I am?" She responded gently, "No, but if you go up to that desk over there and ask them, they will tell you."

Throughout church history, the great deceiver has waged a relentless, highly organized media campaign with one purpose in mind—to keep us believers from understanding who we really are in Christ or what it means to have a relationship with God through Jesus. The funny thing is that he's accomplished it all in a very unlikely place—church.

For almost two millennia, Satan has convinced us that the church is comprised of two groups, the haves and the have-nots; the stars and the rest of us groupies; the ones who are marching to glory and the rest of us who are trying to crawl there; the ones who deserve to be favored and the rest of us who, quite frankly, are lucky to just still be alive; the saints and the rest of us "ain'ts."

In the Roman Church, a highly admired "servant of God" may eventually be declared a saint. Such persons are then canonized, or added to the "canon" or catalog of saints. Their names are invoked at the celebration of the Mass. They are the heroes, the miracle workers. They are infallibly declared by the Pope to be the beautiful people of the church. Because of their great merit, they're even allowed to intercede for the rest of us lowly, average, everyday, run-of-the-mill Christians, who vainly try to gain an audience with God on our own.

In Protestant circles, those who have achieved a measure of prominence are thought to be the "stars" of the faith—the high-octane performers who, because of their latest accomplishment, are given the red carpet treatment, while the rest of us underachievers look for a way in through a side door.

Even in your typical Evangelical church, you'll find a similar delineation. Many will shake their heads in sympathy for their "disillusioned" Catholic friends while they shake their fingers in the faces of their "over-emotional" Pentecostal brethren. And then they will turn around and distribute their own lists of fundamental requirements for God's favor, including the avoidance of certain types of wardrobe styles, cinematic indulgences and, "Lord, have mercy," even utilizing percussion instruments in worship services. All the while, priding themselves as God's favored few while hoping the rest of the church can someday catch on.

YOUR BIGGEST FAN

Yes, we have met the enemy, and they really are us. All of us. We have fallen prey to the deception of the evil one. Having split Christ's body into the few who have "arrived," from the masses who simply try to survive, the deceiver has reduced the self-esteem of the average believer to the point where he or she wonders if there is any hope of ever capturing the elusive butterflies of victory, success and joy. We long for sainthood, but are convinced it is out of reach for us. We might as well get used to it, we will always be playing catch-up. The little engines that can't, right?

Satan paints a pretty bleak picture for us if we want to buy it. I don't, and I suggest you don't either. I suppose it all boils down to who you believe—your biggest enemy or your biggest Fan; a lying father or a loving Father; someone who hopes to destroy you or Someone who has already died for you! Is that a tough choice? Didn't think so.

FOR THE RECORD

In the New Testament God calls the believer a "saint" 62 times. It's true. We are all the *hagioi*, the "set apart ones," the "righteous ones." In Paul's opening remarks to the church at Corinth, he does not address two classes of Christians. He calls all of the believers there "saints." That's right, the struggling church in Corinth was full of divisive, accusatory, immoral believers—but saints, nonetheless. Now, if God says you're on the list, then you're on the list, regardless of what the Pope says.

Every believer, not just a select few, is a "set apart," positionally righteous, fully equipped, high-powered spiritual machine! That is who *you* are! And it's been that way from the first moment you said yes to Jesus Christ. There is no spiritual superstar on any media network, at any church, in any pulpit anywhere who has more spiritual potential than you do at this very moment. We are all the "haves." In Christ, there are no "have-nots." We're all saints. At some point, that reality has to make the eighteen-inch trip from your brain to your heart.

THAT'S THE SPIRIT!

Remember, God doesn't compare us to each other. Even as human parents, we're warned about comparing one of our children to another or trying to motivate one to be more like the other. Never forget the five-talent servant got the same reward as the ten-talent servant. They were judged like we all will be, according to what's been given to us to do and use. And this much can be said of every one of us—on the average, we all have eight to fifteen people that God has strategically and supernaturally placed in our sphere of influence so that He can use us to show them how much He loves them. Accountability to our Master begins there.

There is an abundant life out there. It's for you. There are unbelievable opportunities out there. They're yours. Not just the pastor's, not just the people leading the ministry you attend, but *yours*. Believe it. This is the first step on the road to revival. By the way, that's your revival. Maybe you've never even been "vived" yet, let alone revived. Regardless, we've got to start someplace, and you're the best place I can think of.

In the movie, *The Last Starfighter*, teenager Alex Rogan is recruited to combat intergalactic evil on the other side of the Cosmos:

Alex: "Listen, Centauri, I'm not any of those guys...I'm a kid from a trailer park."

Centauri: "If that's what you think, then that's all you'll ever be!"

Through the years, I've seen so many people dismiss the opportunity to make a difference in their worlds, simply because they don't see themselves like Jesus does. They don't believe that one person can make that big of a difference for the Kingdom of God.

In the climactic scene of the same movie, Alex discovers the fate of the Star League (the good guys) has come down to one final battle. A conversation with his alien copilot reflects the same level of optimism that God feels for each one of us.

Alex: "So...how many Starfighters are left?"

Grig: "Including you?...one."

Alex: "One Gunstar? Against the whole (enemy) Armada? It'll be a slaughter!"

Grig: (With a smile and an enthusiastic fist pump) "That's the spirit!" [1]

"Few things are harder to put up with than the annoyance of a good example!"

CHAPTER 11
PODCASTING CORINTH

We've all dreamed of accomplishing something significant for Jesus. Fame and recognition may fuel the ego, but significance is what counts. I can tell you from experience that being prominent isn't all it appears to be. Think of it this way. My bald head is prominent, but my liver is significant. The difference is critical.

When we set a course for significance in God's Kingdom, we have to look no further than our own oikos to find it. That's where we've been planted, and that's where God expects us to bloom—at least initially. More opportunities may indeed come but, even if they don't, you will always be God's doorway into the hearts and lives of your oikos. That small group of people is like a miniature ballpark and, the smaller the field, the easier it is to hit a home run.

DEFINING SIGNIFICANCE

Earlier, I mentioned the problem of factions in the Corinthian church. The discord that was such a concern to the Apostle Paul did not seem to be the result of divisive leaders. The rift was not even the result of some sort of clash between the leadership styles those guys brought to the table. The problem developed because groups within the church brought too much of their culture into their fellowship. In ancient Greece, it was typical for local philosophers to regularly compete for followers. The Corinthian believers had simply organized their own "Who's the Best Pastor" tournament. It was a blessing that those leaders were not feeding that frenzy or else the debate could have really gotten out of hand!

The church has always faced the challenge of trying to motivate people who believe that significance is defined as simply being a fan of great church leaders. "We just love our church!" Or, "Our pastor is the best!" Or, "We podcast Andy Stanley and John Piper—therefore, we're faithful." There's nothing wrong with loving those guys, but just because we are loyal to a particular local church or fans of a gifted church leader doesn't mean that we are faithful followers of Christ. But that's not a new phenomenon—evidently the Corinthians were the same way. Some said, "I podcast Paul." Others, "I podcast Apollos." Still others, "I podcast Peter!"

Henri Tajfel and John Turner put the discussion of *Social Identity Theory* on the modern psychological map by proposing different mental processes involved in evaluating others as "us." They were intrigued by the emotional significance that seems to depend on identifying with a famous individual or group and how our self-esteem actually becomes bound to that group identity. [1]

But why is that? Why is identifying with the celebrity of others so important to us? Maybe we wish we could sing well but, since we can't, we become fans of the superstar who has the voice we wish we had. We can't hit baseballs 400 feet but we can root for someone who can, someone who can do what we wish we could.

And maybe it isn't much different at church—we don't feel like we could, in and of ourselves, ever make much of a dent in a pagan culture and identifying with a high impact celebrity ministry gives us that chance. We don't feel like we can ever make much of a difference for the Kingdom, so we cheer for someone who already is! But Paul's letter to the Corinthians was pretty clear—we cannot sit on the sideline and just root for a Christian celebrity, whoever our personal spiritual mentor happens to be, without considering the implications of our own mission.

The leadership team at any local church cannot make an impact on a community without the personal participation of the church family. For example, you can sit in one of our auditoriums week after week and listen to people like me talk about God, but any impact that we leaders might have is contingent on you taking that information to the people that God has supernaturally and strategically placed in your sphere of influence. Those people are probably not going to believe us pastors anyway—from their vantage point, we're paid to say this stuff. And that's the church most of us grew up in, where the paid clergy talked about God's character but the people never seemed to connect the dots between their personal growth and their personal mission. It's an important pathway, that from podcast to purpose—unfortunately, a path less followed every day.

THE GREATEST POSSIBLE IMPACT

So, Tom, "We get saved and then God gives us a job to do?" No, this is not a job description, it's a paradigm transformation!

What we sometimes don't realize is that we are witnessing for Him all the time. Every encounter we have, every word we speak, every action we take is a direct demonstration of His presence in our lives. We can't avoid it. Our oikos will make assumptions and draw their own conclusions. At times, they won't be able to avoid drawing the wrong ones. But light is what it is—as we remain intentional in our role, good things will happen.

A man once counseled his son that if he wanted to live a long life, the secret was to sprinkle a little gunpowder on his cornflakes every morning. The son did this religiously, and he lived to the ripe old age of 93. When he died, he left 14 children, 28 grandchildren, 35 great-grandchildren, and a 15-foot hole in the wall of the crematorium. That's impact!

Our households continue to be the arenas where our testimonies can have the greatest possible impact. Why is that? Because your life lived out in front of your oikos demonstrates your faith—whether you want it to or not, whether you think it does or not. We naturally have more quality opportunities to share with the people we are with most often.

A NEW SET OF KEYS

Nothing says "I've arrived" quite like a teenager's first car. Since I turned 16 just a few months before my high school graduation, *my* quest for a first car was especially significant—most of my classmates had already been driving for two years and my social life needed a boost. All that to say, when my friend, Rick, told me that his '57 Chevy was for sale, I begged him to hold onto it until my father could come by and look at it. Even though I had saved up the $300 asking price and had a part-time job to cover ancillary expenses, I knew my dad would need to weigh in before the deal could be closed!

I'll never forget the night that we drove out to Rick's place to see the car. My heart was beating so fast I could actually hear it! Dad took a long look at the Chevy and said, "I don't think it's the car for you." I tried to protest, but it was clear he wasn't going to budge. I remember the ride home being pretty quiet. In fact, I don't think I spoke to my dad for the better part of the week.

Five days later, he walked in my room (uninvited). I thought I was going to get a sermon on the importance of respecting your parents. But instead, he threw the keys to a '69 Mustang with a 351-Cleveland V-8 on my bed. "I've been working on a deal for a Mustang for the last month—I didn't want to say anything because I wanted to surprise you."

High gloss cherry red, fastback, rear *Highjacker* air-shocks, 8-track stereo sound system, oversized white letter custom wheels and, to top it all off, air-conditioning. Air-conditioning! This was 1970—no one my age drove an air-conditioned car! In one minute's time, I went from an academic nerd (which in my world hadn't yet delivered many perks) to driving not only one of the fastest, and not just one of the most beautiful, but also one of the coolest (literally) cars anywhere!

You need to understand, my father was an associate pastor at a Baptist church. He just didn't make that kind of money. To this day, I'm not sure how he landed that car. (Would it be overstating the obvious to say that I started speaking to him again shortly after that?)

I learned a lot that week about a father's love, but I also learned something else. From the first moment I picked up those keys, I knew my life had changed—and it wasn't just that I finally had a car that would get me, as they say, from here to there. Those keys gave me opportunities for social access that had eluded me to that point. Evidently, I instantly became more interesting, more articulate and better looking! Obviously, none of those things were actually true—who I was didn't change, but how people perceived me shifted in a big way.

That's what happens in an oikos. You could have a high level of integrity while living all by yourself. But in a social setting, with people living close enough to see who you really are, whatever integrity you already had is now generating conversations, providing respect and elevating influence.

In 1 Peter 3, the Apostle throws us a set of keys, enabling

us to inject new energy into our personal growth that, in turn, elevates our personal mission. Pick these keys up and you'll have more opportunities for worldchange than you ever thought possible.

KEY #1: Your life sparks the interest of your oikos.

The question of what to do as a Christian has always been overshadowed by who you are. While evangelistic technique is a helpful study, the best way to prepare for effective evangelism is to simply mature in your faith.

"But in your hearts revere Christ as Lord. Always be prepared to give an answer to everyone who asks you to give the reason for the hope that you have." (1 Peter 3:15a)

That sequence is pretty simple: Your growth leads to their interest, which leads to their questions, which lead to your answers.

KEY #2: Your life silences the criticism of your oikos.

One of the more frustrating things we've always had to contend with is the criticism of ignorant people. The general perception of the Christian faith is regularly manipulated by the media. If given any consideration at all, the voice of faith on a panel or the "Christian" character in a cast seems to always be framed as either bitter, judgmental or hypocritical. As unfair or unfortunate as that may be, few of us can do much about the general public's perception of Christianity. We'll probably never own a movie studio. But we can make a dent in those perceptions inside one unique circle of relationships. Use words whenever appropriate, but never underestimate the clarity that comes from a faithful life.

"But do this with gentleness and respect, keeping a clear conscience, so that those who speak maliciously against your good behavior in Christ may be ashamed of their slander." (1 Peter 3:15b-16)

KEY #3: Your life establishes the validity of your message.

A Ford salesman who tells you to come by and see him because the greatest vehicle in the world is made by Ford, and then waves as he drives away in a Toyota will probably not get your business. Neither will someone who preaches about God but lives like the Devil.

Susan's story makes the point. "I grew up in a home without faith, but it never really bothered me. I bounced around, attending different churches and listening to different people explain different beliefs. Tony was different—he would always tell me about his faith, about how Jesus saved him and that He could do the same for me. He invited me to church where the pastor spoke about the oikos, and why God put those people in my life. I realized that Jesus had used my oikos to bring me there for a reason, and that reason was to be saved. After listening to the rest of the message, I prayed right there in church and asked Jesus to come into my life."

Aristotle said: "Persuasion is achieved by the speaker's personal character when the speech is so spoken as to make us think him credible. We believe good men more readily than others: This is true generally whatever the question is, and absolutely true where exact certainty is impossible and opinions are divided...his character may almost be called the most effective means of persuasion he possesses." [2]

Mark Twain was a bit grumpier. "Few things are harder to put up with than the annoyance of a good example!" [3]

A faith demonstration is so powerful, it transcends technology. Read the following testimony from Shelly, who was impacted by someone 2,500 miles away!

"I was friends with a girl from an online pregnancy club when she discovered her baby's life was terminal. I watched as she remained faithful to God and asked her about her faith. After months of encouragement, she found HDC online (she lives in Indiana) and told me to try this church. When I walked in, I immediately felt like I belonged and kept coming back. After two services, I accepted Christ. That was one and a half years ago and I'm still on fire for God."

By the way, Shelley's husband has since also given his life to Christ.

EASY ASSIMILATION

Another reason the oikocentric lifestyle is so effective is because new believers are more easily assimilated into the life of a church. It's a fact—they will have family or good friends who are already involved in the church *before* they get there. They naturally feel at home as soon as they arrive! Can you think of a more effective welcoming strategy than providing newcomers with their own personal concierge?

We've all heard the TV infomercials declare, "But wait, there's more!" Well, the bonus here is when people come to faith because of someone in their oikos they are much more likely to take the same good news to the other members of their oikos. The oikocentric lifestyle is not just organic and non-threatening, it's self-replicating! It's not too much for a new believer to understand because they have just experienced how it works. It feels natural to them.

"But, Tom, I was raised a Christian and my family and friends are already believers—so who's in my oikos?" That's a great question, and the next one I want to consider.

*"The love of Christ propagates the way
zombies do in a scary movie... By contact!"*

CHAPTER 12
THE DANCE CARD

Before my time, there was a popular custom in polite society. When at a dance, each gal would have what was called a "dance card." When a guy would ask her for a dance, she would write his name on her dance card so she would know who her partner would be for each dance. Considered rather silly in the social networking culture we live in today, those dance cards have now been consigned to scrapbooks and memorabilia boxes. But society back then had more uniform rules than it does now. People were expected to interact with their friends, neighbors and families according to certain customs.

In our culture, the amount of contact we have with those same groups is quite a bit less and seems more superficial. Years ago, people would always acknowledge one another as they walked by, even if they'd never met. But today we train our children to avoid them, to "never speak to strangers." We build walls around our homes and don't get out of the car until the garage door is closed safely behind us. We have become a society of isolated people. Most social networking occurs behind the veil of a computer screen.

Yet, there are still those eight to fifteen people with whom we do life—those with whom we regularly come into contact. They could be relatives, friends, neighbors, classmates, co-workers, or others we encounter on a regular basis. These are the people who belong on our dance cards, if you will.

Believe me, people are generally more needy and lonely than ever. Some might be easy to share with and others will find it tough getting over their wall of self-isolation, but people have never been hungrier for relationships or more afraid of them.

SCALING THE WALL

Do the unexpected. One of our members told me about rolling a trash can back up the driveway for his elderly neighbor because he knew it was a bit of a struggle for her. He didn't wait to be asked and she didn't know he was being helpful until several weeks later. One day she finally saw it was him and that led to a new level of conversations.

Just be yourself. You don't have to act like a street evangelist unless you are one. Just be who you are. Your personality works the best for you, so don't adopt someone else's. You don't have to know all the answers, you just have to authentically care and not be afraid to let it show.

Never underestimate the power of nice. Sometimes people get so scuffed up by the world, all it takes is someone being nice to them to get their attention. The Bible says that even God's kindness is intended to lead people to repentance. (Romans 2:4)

Be more consistent. I'm going to give you six things in the next section that you can do for your oikos. Do them consistently and you will be stunned at how the Lord will use you to demonstrate His love to your oikos. After all, He's the One who placed them in your life.

Be more persistent. Just because someone says no the first time you ask them to come to church with you doesn't mean they won't ever say yes. If the Lord knows He can count on you to be gently persistent, then He can arrange an invitation from you to coincide with a felt need of theirs.

Oh, one more—listen to the voice of the Holy Spirit. As you move into this oikocentric lifestyle you will find more and more that you're hearing that small whisper guiding you. This is very important—listen to it.

This book is about how God uses regular people to leverage Kingdom work. Most of them don't do big things and, whatever they do, they do for or with people they've already known a while. How hard is that? It may seem uncomfortable at first, but you know what? After a while it becomes a very engaging and natural lifestyle.

HOW TO USE YOUR DANCE CARD

STEP #1: Make a list.

I know that seems a bit elementary, but it is the first key step in being effective within your oikos. It's sort of like the old Irish recipe for rabbit stew. "First, catch the rabbit." If you don't know who is in your oikos, you won't follow through with the other five steps very effectively. So paint the target.

The longer you've been a Christian, the fewer non-believers will make your first draft. I actually have people tell me that they don't really know any non-Christians, but that's because no one has ever trained them to think in an oikocentric way. We are all more connected to non-believers than we realize. Only a lack of intentionality keeps our focus inward, provoking the natural instinct to surround ourselves by other Christians who can minister to us rather than focusing outward, to the relationships that frame our God given purpose.

As your journey continues, you will gradually see your world more clearly through those new non-glare oikos lenses you're now sporting. You will begin to see many of the relationships that you once took for granted as the divine connections they actually are. You will stop seeing others through the limited perspective of your own interests—what others can provide *you*. Rather you'll start seeing them through the eyes of God—what you can actually provide *them*.

WHO makes up **YOUR** 8-15?
Relatives
Friends
Neighbors
WorkAssociates
Classmates
others

First, list your "oikos," those 8-15 people with whom you interact regularly.

1. _____
2. _____
3. _____
4. _____
5. _____
6. _____
7. _____
8. _____
9. _____
10. _____
11. _____
12. _____
13. _____
14. _____
15. _____

Then, make a commitment to pray daily for your "world." Pray that each one would sense God's presence in their lives and that God would draw each one closer to Himself. Offer yourself everyday as an instrument in that process. Watch for appropriate opportunities to discuss and demonstrate your faith in Christ, as well as invite them to church.

Most people look for a hairdresser simply to fix their hair. Not Myndi! She reflected on the development of that relationship, "My hairdresser and I exchanged phone numbers because we had a lot in common. One night, a few months later, we were going to church together and she and her husband accepted Christ at the end of the service."

As awesome as that sounds, listen to how those events unfolded from Lynsey's perspective. "I'm a hairdresser, and one of my clients invited my husband and me to church. We were hesitant at first—we had struggled with infertility for a few years and were running out of hope, so we decided we had nothing to lose. After we attended the young adult service for the first time, we wanted more. We faithfully started going to church and learning about God. About six months later, we discovered we were going to have triplets! We gave our lives to God and have been blessed with three healthy sons. Now we can't wait to tell them what God has done in our lives."

You might want to group the people on your list by different categories such as family, work, school, etc. But one thing they all have in common is that they'll all be a part of your schedule in the foreseeable future—so consider your calendar a prayer journal!

You'll also find that different spiritual categories are represented. Some are non-believers. They need to be *evangelized*—they need Christ. Some are believers who have allowed other important challenges of life to crowd out the most important one, preparing to be worldchangers—they need to be *energized* for a purpose-driven mission. Some are believers already focused on becoming better prepared to reach out to their own oikos for Christ—they need to be *encouraged* to stay the course.

Two points here—(1) recognize who is in your world and (2) remember that everyone in it needs your appropriate input and support.

STEP #2: Keep it current.

Remember, you're listing, not choosing. They've already been chosen for you—every member of your oikos has been supernaturally and strategically placed in your relational world. You may not even like some of those people, but that's irrelevant. Just because you wouldn't have selected them doesn't mean they're going anywhere! We all dream of inter-oikos transfers, from time to time, but to no avail. As people wander in and out of your oikos, you'll notice that their migratory patterns are not so much the result of your personal magnetism as they are the result of divinely orchestrated circumstances.

You'll be surprised at how fluid your oikos will become. There will be some who never leave your list, others who come and go, and still others who will lead you to even more others! Your oikos will grow. Don't worry if you only start out with five or so. The Lord will bring the right people to your mind, those who should be included and those who should be released. Keeping your oikos list current will keep you both aware of and focused on your mission. Your oikos list is also a great reminder of your world's fluidity. Those windows of opportunity do not remain open forever. People move away. People change jobs. People die.

STEP #3: Pray everyday for your entire oikos.

If you think that's too simplistic, think again! The Bible couldn't be clearer—our prayers bring a level of supernatural power to the process that cannot be accessed any other way. And it's not because God needs to be regularly reminded of how important and needy those people are—we do! Your continual awareness of their presence and your ability to recognize opportunities to reach out to them will increase if you're praying for them everyday. Your usefulness will increase. Your availability will increase because your attitude will change. You will begin to see those people the way God sees them— dearly loved and desperately needing Him.

I suggest that you not only pray for their needs, but also pray for opportunities to share with them. Notice, I didn't say just share the Gospel with them. You may well have the opportunity to do that (after all, ultimately, that is the point), but often it is just the fact that someone they know truly cares about them and is praying for them that will open their hearts to the Gospel. Praying for your oikos is the most powerful, spiritual and practical thing you can do for them!

STEP #4: Invite them to church regularly.

Notice the word *invite*. It should be a gracious invitation. We are not here to judge people simply because they haven't been attending. Also, the invitation should be extended regularly. Who knows when you, like Myndi, might catch them at a point in life where their need is larger than their fear? You just never know.

STEP #5: Prepare to both clearly display God's character and defend your faith in Jesus.

This is where both personal and corporate discipleship strategies kick in. Only now, we're not growing in our faith to pat ourselves on the back. We've embraced true discipleship by preparing to change our world!

STEP #6: Be accountable to others for steps 1 through 5.

Christianity is a team sport. Being part of a small accountability group will help to keep you on task. When you start praying for your respective oikos networks with others, you may discover that several of your group's oikos cards have some of the same entries. That's when things really get interesting, as two or more people intentionally prepare to reach out to the same individual or family.

LOVE AS A VIRUS

After Pastor Kevin Reynolds issued the oikos challenge to his congregation at Flipside Church in Rancho Cucamonga, California, he received the following e-mail. Dale's comments reflect a common plight:

"I had a little trouble filling out my oikos card when I first received it. There were these little blank slots on the back of the card where I could write the names of people I dealt with regularly. They had category titles above them—family, school, work. Pastor Kev explained that these prayers would be the first step toward creating a deeper connection and caring between me and those people. I gave it some thought and penciled in a few names...the nephew who wanted to talk about God at a recent family gathering...the coworker who, out of the blue, recently asked me if I believed...my wife who had been having a minor but annoying health problem.

But the stupid card had yet more slots and more categories—church, neighborhood, extra curricular, other. Extra curricular? Other? What does this little card want from me, blood? I penciled in a few more names...the Christian brother who had drifted away from faith...the neighbor who gently but persistently mocked my church-going ways and his wife who had chronic pain. I filled in as many slots as I could and I started to pray for those people.

Kev had cautioned us not to let this become a guilt thing, not to worry if we missed a day. He said that no one was keeping score and, for a while, it would be hit and miss. Some days they would completely slip my mind. Other days, I'd tack their concerns onto the end of my daily prayers.

Then I noticed something began to happen to me. The process reversed itself...changed up. I'd think of one of these people and their problems or their needs during the course of a day and that would prompt me to stop for a moment and pray for them specifically. I wasn't just giving someone else a little space in my prayer time, I was devoting extra time outside of my normal prayer schedule to pray specifically for them. And what's more, I began to care more about these people, to take an active interest in their lives. I even began to expect my prayers to get results. I thought some more about this weird oikos concept and came up with a few metaphors of my own. It occurred to me that God designed the Gospel to spread like a virus in an international airport...from one person to two more to four more to dozens more...and then those dozens all get on planes and take it with them to their home countries. The love of Christ propagates the way zombies do in a scary movie, I thought, by contact. Salvation spreads like a juicy rumor from person to person to people around the world. So, with this love-as-a-virus idea in my head, I continued to add people to my oikos list...my sister who needed Christ, and a job... my brother who wasn't saved...a friend at church who had a non-life threatening but chronic and sometimes painful disease. I added a friend from an internet message board I frequent who practices what he calls 'Christian mysticism,' then realized that if I added him I'd better also add the guy from the same board I don't much care for because he makes me mad.

So, frankly, this whole oikos thing is getting out of hand. It's a nice idea, but it's snowballing on me!"

THE CHURCH'S ROLE

In an oikocentric church the major purpose for social events is to serve as opportunities to bring members of your oikos to the church under less intimidating circumstances. We have an annual men's BBQ event and, each year, I fully expect a large portion of the guys to be first timers from our men's oikos networks. We have a clean comedy night once a year with the same purpose—invite your oikos. In fact, we encourage our people to buy more tickets than they have immediate family members just so they will be motivated to invite members of their oikos.

Our annual summer children's emphasis welcomes tons of kids every year, and many of them were invited by other kids—

because every child has eight to fifteen children whom God has supernaturally and strategically placed in their worlds too. Even the regular worship services are deliberately structured to attract and minister to people brought there by someone in their oikos.

The church is not only a place to train believers in personal growth, it becomes a partner in their personal mission—in the actual process of introducing non-believing members of oikos networks to Jesus. A church that finds that groove, operating naturally and comfortably according to the model laid out by the Head of the church is a very cool thing. It's also pretty rare.

PART 3:
CONCENTRATING ON PEOPLE

"They've got him-credible witnesses, documents, Heaven knows what else. In all my years as a prosecutor, I've never seen such an open-and-shut case."

CHAPTER 13
THE ESSENCE OF EVANGELISM

God has never expected us to cram His truth down anyone's throats. We are simply His mouthpiece as He works in the hearts of others, creating in them the desire to ask the right questions. We are simply the witnesses. If we do our job, He'll put the case together.

I grew up watching *Perry Mason*, the original television courtroom drama. Perry didn't always win but, in the end, it seemed he always managed to vindicate the innocent and expose the guilty. Later came *Matlock*, *LA Law* and *The Practice*.

And, now, entire television networks are dedicated to the work that goes on in the courtroom—always dramatic, lives hanging in the balance, mystery, controversy and, hopefully, justice.

The Bible is full of that kind of stuff. It is, essentially, a divine deposition. In the Old Testament, the Law takes center stage— the first five Books of the Old Testament are referred to as the Books of the Law. The historical record that follows reads like a rap sheet. The prophets speak of certain judgment. In the New Testament, Jesus pays for our capital crimes and delivers us from the eventual verdict of eternal death.

Visualize that courtroom with me.

God would certainly sit behind the bench. He is referred to as the Source of justice, the Judge of the living and the dead.

In the defendant's seat, we would find Jesus. He is on trial. He made claims so sensational that His enemies were bound and determined to execute Him. And that's the question all of us must eventually face. Was He telling the truth or was He a con, guilty of perpetuating the greatest fraud in human history?

On the other side of the aisle, we find Satan. He is the prosecutor. In fact, the word, "Devil," comes from the Greek, diablos, which means accuser, or slanderer.

The Holy Spirit, on the other hand, is the chief Defender of the Accused. But while He fights for the honor of His Client, those who are left to render a verdict are feeling a bit guilty themselves.

Sitting along the wall, we find the jury, or as we have come to know them, our oikos. While they try to understand who is telling the truth and who is lying, the simple presence of holiness in the courtroom has now placed them on the defensive. At some point, as their decision about Jesus is rendered and, as they finally come to grips with who He is, it will be up to each of them to admit their own guilt. That's the kind of bombshell that every season finale is looking for...at that culminating moment, all eyes are on the bench, the Accused is declared innocent, and the jury is exposed as the guilty ones!

Which brings us to the only chair left—the one in which the witness sits, the one you and I presently occupy. We used to be members of the jury, but that was before we became believers. Now, we occupy the witness box. It's never been a witness' job to convince the jury of anything. The lawyers get paid the big bucks to do that. But that doesn't take away this all-important role of being witnesses—those who simply tell what they know about the Accused.

So, like it or not, we are now on the spot. The Holy Spirit calls out. "I'd like to call Tom Mercer to the witness stand!" What will I say when the accuser grills me? What will I say when the Defender prompts me to respond? What kind of witness will I be for Jesus? Good? Bad? Or just plain ugly? And we can ill afford to leave the room because, eventually, the Defender will call on each one of us.

That reality should not intimidate us. The prosecutor might like us to believe that we are responsible to convince someone that they should place their faith in Christ, but nothing could be further from the truth. But why would Satan want us to think we have to be the convincers? It drains our confidence. Our fear of failure gives him leverage. That heavy of a burden will keep us from ever stepping out to verbalize our faith. The good news is we don't have to convince anyone—we are merely the witnesses.

We have no choice but to be witnesses. We don't go out to do witnessing. That kind of terminology has led to wrong ideas about sharing our faith. It's not something we *do*. It's someone we *are*.

"But you will receive power when the Holy Spirit comes on you; and you will be my witnesses in Jerusalem, and in all Judea and Samaria, and to the ends of the earth." (Acts 1:8)

BEING PREPARED

God will use us to testify to anything and everything that we have prepared to share. The more we understand about His Word, the better able He will be to call on us at anytime. If we only know a little, He can only use us to say a little. Oikos brings new energy to the discipline of studying the Scriptures. We no longer learn the Word to simply expand our neural capacity or impress our Christian friends or church leaders. We learn with a purpose, that we might describe the full counsel of God to our relational worlds.

In John 9, the blind man didn't know much. He hadn't yet had the time to learn about Jesus. But he did tell what he knew.

"Whether he (Jesus) is a sinner or not, I don't know. One thing I do know. I was blind but now I see." (John 9:25)

That was the extent of his testimony, because that was the extent of his experience with Christ. And no matter what level of doctrine you understand, you will always have the story of *your* experience with Christ, what He has done in your life. At some point it will become a powerful part of virtually every evangelistic conversation you have, so you might as well think about it now.

Many Christians have never taken the time to think through the testimony of their experience with Christ. Yours could probably be explained in a few statements. Given the chance, those few statements might evolve into a more detailed presentation. Depending on the setting, the length and specifics might vary.

But every version should include three elements, so let's take a look at them. I encourage you to fill in the blanks in the next section. Don't worry about someone else reading it when you loan this book to a friend. Sharing yourself and what Jesus has done for you is what this is all about. Give this some thought because your story will add a sense of authenticity to whatever biblical truths are relevant to your oikos. Here are the basic three elements of a testimony. Give it a shot.

PART #1: Your prior dissatisfaction

What caused you to see that you had a need for Jesus Christ? Was it an event, a tragedy, a church program?

_____

_____

_____

_____

PART #2: Your conversion experience

Where did you actually pray to give your life to Christ? When was that? Were others present?

_____

_____

_____

_____

PART #3: The benefits of your salvation

What one or two things have you discovered to be the greatest benefits of knowing Christ?

_____

_____

_____

_____

In addition to our story, we also have two other weapons at our disposal: the powerful tool of the Word of God and the voice of the Holy Spirit living in us.

"All Scripture is God-breathed and is useful for teaching, rebuking, correcting and training in righteousness, so that the servant of God may be thoroughly equipped for every good work." (2 Timothy 3:16-17) And that includes evangelism!

1 Peter 3:15 calls for us to, "Always be prepared to give an answer to everyone who asks you to give the reason for the hope that you have."

You never know who will ask; you never know what they will ask; and you never know when you're talking to a dying man. But we aren't without help in this regard.

"The Advocate, the Holy Spirit, whom the Father will send in my name, will teach you all things and will remind you of everything I have said to you." (John 14:26)

The promise that we will be given the words with which to testify presumes that we have already taken the time and made the effort to learn those things in God's Word. That's why our understanding of how those two work together is vital. With our story in place, an ever-increasing understanding of the Word of God in our hearts, and an ear tuned to the voice of the Holy Spirit, we develop the ability to respond to the needs of those around us, regardless of the specific need. We can effectively testify to what we know. And our testimony will be powerful.

When people hear the word "scandal" regarding the Nixon Administration, they immediately think of *Watergate*. As big a threat as that posed to his presidency, it wasn't the only legal difficulty Nixon faced. Five years into his presidency, his Vice President, Spiro Agnew was indicted for tax fraud and extortion. As the U.S. Attorney General during those years, Elliot Richardson appraised the government's case against the Vice President this way. "They've got him—credible witnesses, documents, Heaven knows what else. In all my years as a prosecutor, I've never seen such an open-and-shut case." [1] And that is exactly the kind of confidence we can bring to our mission every day! Credible witnesses, the greatest Document in history and the Heavenly knowledge of the Holy Spirit...add it all up and you've got worldchange!

TIMING IS POWER

Testifying about the love and power of God is easy for us when all is well. In fact, testimonies of God's faithfulness are expected when everyone's healthy and all the bills are paid. Ironically enough, though, it is during those times that the world is least interested in trusting Christ. They may not even be watching.

However, turn on the faith in a time of crisis, and the world is mesmerized, dumb-founded. They cannot, for the life of them, figure out the power of contentment in times of difficulty. The impact is profound, because it takes them totally by surprise.

"Three times I pleaded with the Lord to take it (a physical infirmity, a 'messenger of Satan') away from me. But he said to me, 'My grace is sufficient for you, for my power is made perfect in weakness.' Therefore I will boast all the more gladly about my weaknesses, so that Christ's *power* may rest on me." (2 Corinthians 12:8-9)

While many in the church only brag about God in times of healing or prosperity, Paul bragged about God in the midst of an illness that God remained silent about, despite the Apostle's continuous prayers for deliverance.

What about you? Have you ever given God an opportunity to use you in a difficult time? What was the result?

Understand, difficulty is not something we long for by any means. It is in no way spiritual to ask for trouble. That's a perversion of faith. But difficult times will inevitably come, so when they show up, don't overlook the wonderful opportunities they offer you to be used by God in such a powerful way. There are times when you're going to be sick or unemployed or up against the wall somehow for as long as God allows anyway, so you might as well take advantage of it!

Julie would tell you that, to be a worldchanger in your sphere of relationships, you need to be prepared to be the agent of change when the opportunity presents itself, in the best of times as well as the worst.

"Our neighbors, Rich and Carol, were two of our closest friends. Although they let us bring their children to church with us, they wouldn't come themselves. We prayed for them to know Christ personally and for God to use us in any way He could.

One day, my husband, Monte, took our children up to the mountains for a picnic and short hike, leaving me at home to catch up with some housework. Their short hike turned into a very long night. They got lost. Everybody didn't have cell phones back then, so I found out they were missing when a park ranger called and said they had found my car still parked in the visitor's center lot after closing. I called our youth pastor and his wife and our neighbors, Rich and Carol, and we all went up to the ranger's station.

We prayed and waited and waited and prayed. After six hours, my fears got the best of me and I broke down and cried out to God. Our youth pastor prayed that the wind would guide the search team to my family. Thirty minutes later we heard that they had been found, and that the ranger who found them had held up his finger and decided to look in whatever direction the wind blew. Rich and Carol witnessed God's amazing power that night. Within a couple of weeks, they both made the decision to follow Christ. They have been actively involved in our church ever since!"

"An empowered organization is one in which individuals have the knowledge, skill, desire and opportunity to personally succeed in a way that leads to collective organizational success."

CHAPTER 14
AS SIMPLE AS A-B-C

Remember the dance card? Well, when people in your oikos see your life of faith lived out before them, they will be curious. Sometimes their internal question will be, "What does he have that I don't have?" Or "How can she be so happy when things are so difficult for her?" Whatever causes them to look to you as dealing with life better than they do, it is the nature of your relationship with them that will fortify the bridge between you and allow them the freedom to speak honestly.

Let's look again at where these people are in relationship to you. Here's a diagram to help you group them.

That's you in the center there, looking like a star! Not to make it all about us, but the star analogy is not that far-fetched. You are certainly being watched. You shine brightly in their world against a dark backdrop of frustration and futility. You're a source of light for them and, finally, just like people still wish upon a star, they will sometimes look to you in desperation for help. In a seemingly impossible situation they will know that God is their only hope, and that you just might be the one He will use to illuminate the way.

So we come now to the crux of the matter. Here is where the rubber meets the road. You're having a conversation with a member of your oikos and after a pause they ask you, "So, how does someone become a Christian?" You've been waiting a long time to have this conversation, but you can feel the butterflies in your stomach struggling to get into formation. You know that whatever you say or do next is important. So, whatever it is, you better not blow it, right?

A LESSON LEARNED

Back when I was in high school, my dad had a hairline similar to mine. He used to say that God gave him a crew cut but the crew bailed out! Dad would grow his hair a little longer on the sides so, when he got out of bed every day, his Brylcreemed hair sticking sideways actually made him look a little scary walking down the hallway. That's why I'll never forget what I'm going to tell you next.

He got a phone call late one night from one of our youth group sponsors, Bob Bowman, and the conversation went something like this.

"Pastor Frank? Mike wants to receive Christ." (Mike was a girl—I remember her name because you just don't meet many girls named Mike.)

"Well, go ahead and pray with her," dad said.

"Pastor Frank, I don't know how. You gotta come over!"

Dad sensed the urgency in Bob's voice so he got dressed and drove across town to meet with them. Mike indeed did give her heart to Christ, and dad later came home and went back to bed. But the memory of being just a little bit frightened by the "killer clown" walking down the hallway has stuck with me all these years.

Later on, I heard Bob's testimony. "After Mike received Christ and Pastor Frank had gone back home," he said, "I fell down on my knees and in tears I told God, 'I promise you, Lord, this will never happen again. Next time, I will be ready to lead someone to Christ myself!'"

Bob was the head of the science department at our high school and served as a sponsor in our youth group. Later on he became a youth pastor and, in fact, followed in my dad's footsteps at that same church. Following that, he went into cross-cultural ministries and enjoyed a wonderful career with New Tribes Mission in South America. God did an amazing work in Bob's life, and I still consider him one of my life mentors.

"An empowered organization is one in which individuals have the knowledge, skill, desire and opportunity to personally succeed in a way that leads to collective organizational success." [1] Steven Covey said that—but replace the word, "organization," with the word, "church," and Jesus could have said it!

When somebody in their oikos asks, "How do I become a Christian?" I don't want any of the people in our church to have to say, "Let me call Pastor Tom." I wouldn't have enough time in my day to talk to all of them. Now, don't think I wouldn't try to find time because, of course, I would—but that's not the point. In even a moderately sized church, it's impossible for the pastor to be available to everyone all the time.

The lesson is clear. It is the church's job "to equip his people for works of service, so that the body of Christ may be built up." (Ephesians 4:12)

THE A-B-C'S

Having a personal relationship with Christ is like having a relationship with anyone else. Knowing *about* Him is not the same as knowing Him personally. Sometimes God has to lead us down a painful path before we get to the point where we recognize our need for Him. That can be difficult but, once we arrive there, the next step of placing our faith in Jesus becomes very natural. We close every weekend service at HDC with the same Gospel invitation, involving the same simple approach. We not only want to help people come to a saving faith in Christ, we also want to reinforce for them how to lead members of their oikos to Christ, whenever and wherever the occasion arises.

Every member of HDC's teaching team speaks to believers every weekend. Saying that, however, requires an explanation. We are fully aware that some, perhaps even many in attendance are still pre-Christian, but we put our messages together as if we could assume that everybody in that room is not only a believer but one who wants to know how to better prepare themselves to reach out to their oikos. However, at the end of every message, we add a challenge that goes something like this. "If you have not yet come to know Christ personally, here at High Desert Church we talk about the ABC's of coming to faith." Without short-selling the profound reality of spiritual regeneration, we want to present the components of salvation in a simple and transferable way. Here is the essence of that challenge.

A—ADMIT that you are a sinner who needs a Savior. Owning up to our sin describes the Greek concept of confession. That's the meaning of the word *homologeo* (Gr.), "to agree with." So when you confess, you're agreeing with God that you're not just a sinner but that your sin has placed you in eternal jeopardy. At some point, every one of us has to reach a point where we finally admit that.

B—BELIEVE that Jesus is the only Savior available. The Bible says that salvation is found in no one else. No one else! If you need someone to save you from your failures (and we all do), you'll draw from a short list of candidates. A really short list. Many others may have made the claim, but there is only one bona fide Savior—Jesus. You need to believe that.

C—CHOOSE to follow Christ, to place your faith in Him

alone. Repentance (*metanoia*, Gr.) requires that you make a conscious choice, actually change your mind about the way you're going to live the rest of your life. It means that you scoot out of the driver's seat of your life and let Jesus sit there instead.

If you have not yet admitted your sinfulness and you believe that Jesus is the only option that can really save you; if you want to take care of the sin problem in your life, be delivered from it's bondage; and if you have not yet chosen to place your faith in Christ, then I would invite you to do that before you read any further.

"Come follow me," Jesus said, "and I will send you out to fish for people." (Matthew 4:19) Those disciples had been fishing for fish their entire lives. Jesus came along and said, in effect, "You guys are pretty good with those nets. But if you follow me, we'll change the world together!"

That's essentially the same invitation to personally receive Christ that you would hear from me on any given weekend, encouraging people to follow the ABC's. It's simple. It works.

This was Harold's experience. "My son and daughter-in-law invited me to HDC. When I first walked in I said, 'This doesn't look like any church I have ever seen.' And during the sermon I said, 'That's it, this is where I want to be.' Right then and there, on that very first day, I put my trust in Christ as my Lord and Savior. It was during the prayer time at the end of the service, when Pastor Tom walked us through the ABC's that I gave my life to Christ. I remember thinking, 'I should have done this a long time ago!' "

This was David's experience. His story isn't much different. He started attending our church after his young son asked him, "Dad, who is Jesus and why don't we go to church?" Two days later, a family friend invited David and his family to a service. "As I sat in the service and Pastor Tom invited us to pray the ABC's," he recalled, "I asked Jesus to forgive me for all the wrongs in my life, help me to be more Christlike and to bring peace to my family. A calm feeling came over me at that moment and I have never looked back."

If you attend our church for a year, you'll hear that simple Gospel presentation shared at least 52 times. The beauty of it is that people who attend are learning how to share the Gospel without even intending to! At some point it becomes so familiar to them that, when that inevitable moment arrives and they're directly asked that question, they simply respond, "Uumm, well, the Bible talks about A-B-C. The 'A' is for admit you're a sinner, and then believe that Jesus is the only Savior, and then make a choice to follow Him. If you'd like to do that now, I'd be glad to pray with you."

They've heard it so often it just rolls right out of them, and it gives them the opportunity to kind of close the deal, if you will, lead others to take that step and place their faith in Christ.

Take nine-year old Josh's word for it. "I grew up going to church every week. I was the only one of four brothers who was not a Christian, so I wanted to be one too. While wrestling with my dad one day, I asked him how to become a Christian. He told me that I had to admit I was a sinner. He told me to believe in Jesus Christ. He told me to choose to follow God. After we prayed together, I felt better right away. Now God helps me with my problems—like dealing with my brothers!"

Talk about transformation—getting along with your brothers? That isn't just worldchange, most people would consider it a Red Sea class miracle!

"I told him I wasn't tired. He told me, 'No, but the outfielders sure are.'"

OK

CHAPTER 15
THE OIKOCENTRIC CHURCH

You would think I'd be nervous. I even wondered if I'd be nervous, but when I came out on stage that Sunday morning, I wasn't. Here I was, about to introduce a whole new model for doing church to our people, and not even a second thought. I had made the oikos principle part of my teaching from the beginning of my time at HDC, but it was time to take the next step—to begin the process or restructuring the church to support the mission. I had several discussions with our staff, small as it was at the time, and they were totally on board. But now I was standing on the end of the diving board and we were all about to dive into the deep end. This wasn't just a four-kid youth group, this was an entire church. Here we go, I thought, as I started to speak.

That was years ago. I didn't know then how the Lord would use this model to grow His church, or how it would impact everything we would do, I just believed it had to! We quickly learned that His vision was broader and more impactful than ours. We frequently had to run to catch up with what He was doing, and a big part of our challenge had to do with how we made decisions. Some time-honored programs and systems had to go because they didn't move the mission forward. We had to trust the Lord like never before because we had to surrender some of the control we were used to having. Now ministry would truly be in the hands of the church family.

DAVY CROCKETT WAS RIGHT

Davy had a motto, "Be sure you're right, then go ahead." That sort of sums up how I felt standing on that stage that day. I presented the essence of what you've already read in this book and then reinforced it over the next several months. Eventually the church family understood it well enough to know if they wanted to be on board or not. I actually challenged them, "We are going to be an oikocentric church and, if that's not the kind of church you want to be a part of, I know of several other churches I can refer you to, because I think we're going to need your seat!"

Saying that didn't even feel awkward. I was just trying to clarify what the future would look like. We had drawn a line in the sand. It was what some have called a "quality decision"—one about which you give yourself no further choice and from which there is no retreat. I didn't want anyone to think that oikos was a program or a campaign, lest they come back and ask, "Pastor, I loved the oikos emphasis, now what's next?" They needed to know that there would be no *next!*

What we didn't know at the time was all the rethinking we would have to do about the various elements of "doing church" that up to then we had taken for granted. We had to peel away the layers of the traditional "feed me and give me" mentality and craft a whole new set of "make me and send me" priorities and values, based on an oikocentric way of seeing the world. Rome wasn't built in a day either, but everything changed when we put on that new set of lenses and began to view the world through the eyes of Jesus.

DESIGN AND FUNCTION

As we developed this new model for how we would do

church, we quickly realized that how we designed the structure of our ministry systems would greatly influence how effective their function would be. Design and function are inextricably connected. Our goal was to cooperate with how Jesus designed the church, because the design of anything reflects how the designer values a particular function.

The church must train believers to live successfully. To live successfully as a Christ follower means to not only follow His teachings, but also His example—to live an oikocentric life. Jesus poured His life into twelve men, preparing them to change the world. (Actually, twelve is right in the sweet spot between eight and fifteen.) In doing the Father's will, those men were Jesus' focus. But He didn't have long to get them ready. The deadline loomed larger as the Ascension drew closer. Jesus had to communicate to those men what priority elements would frame the redemptive mission of the church. He had to cut to the chase, flesh out the core.

Jim Collins has written extensively about the importance of core values to any organization.[1] He describes how loosely we can use the term and attach it to components of an organization that aren't really core. He details that, in order for any value to be core, it has to be *essential*—anything you didn't really need shouldn't be considered core. It has to be *enduring*—if it wouldn't last, what would be the point of building anything on it? It had to be *guiding*—a core value should be an indelible arrow, showing the way to greatness when more than one good option is available and tough decisions have to be made. And lastly, it had to be *non-compromisable*—that is, we would stick to it, even if the culture punished us for doing so.

Our first challenge, then, was to determine which core values would best enable us to support, teach and model an oikocentric lifestyle. They would have to be the kind of values that would not only frame the ministry of our church, but also be appropriate as the core values for an individual's life—that is, if we expect worldchange to become more than a subtitle on our stationary. Here are the values we have determined, for HDC, are that important.

TRUTHFUL

"Yet a time is coming and has now come when the true worshipers will worship the Father in spirit and in truth, for they are the kind of worshipers the Father seeks." (John 4:23)

In a post-modern world, truth is defined by each individual and the community of which he or she is a part. That's why it seems as though nothing is certain anymore, that everything is evolving, changing and relative. Worldchangers see things differently. The Bible becomes their stripe clearly marking the centerline of life's road. It is, after all, the inspired, infallible and authoritative Word of God. It is not simply another tool among life's smorgasbord of self-improvement resources. It was given to us as absolute truth—that is, it is true all the time, for everyone in every generation.

"For, 'All people are like grass, and all their glory is like the flowers of the field; the grass withers and the flowers fall, but the word of the Lord endures forever.' And this is the word that was preached to you." (1 Peter 1:24-25)

The Bible speaks with a divine authority and creates a divine empowerment that is unparalleled in any other literature. If you read it and still wonder if it is true, I say, "Try it!" See if applying the principles it contains doesn't change your life from the inside out and make you the kind of person that you've been futilely trying to become without it.

"All Scripture is God-breathed and is useful for teaching, rebuking, correcting and training in righteousness, so that the servant of God may be thoroughly equipped for every good work." (2 Timothy 3:16-17)

The prophet Isaiah declared that everything else might fade away, but the Word of God would always prevail. More than anything else on Earth, what is written there is core. It is essential. It is enduring. It is guiding. And it is non-compromisable.

HELPFUL

You will find that many people in your oikos grew up attending church. Whether their background was Protestant or Roman Catholic, Mormon or otherwise, very few people will be entering a church for the first time when they come to yours! In fact, they were probably faithful attendees for years, having been taken by their parents on most weekends while they were growing up. But, that's the thing, they grew up! They weren't forced to attend any longer and so they stopped. Why? Because the church they grew up in didn't tell them truth? Perhaps, but not likely. At least I don't meet many people who say, "I grew up in church but stopped going because the pastor didn't teach the Bible." The reason they stopped attending was because church wasn't helpful.

As Christians, we need to help people connect dots in their everyday lives between their experiences, their choices and mission critical objectives. Even Christian disciplines become oikocentric.

The discipline of Bible study becomes a strategic process that prepares us to answer questions and provide a biblical perspective of the things people in our oikos experience every day. In addition, we live out the grace-enhancing principles it contains, displaying the character of the One who loves them so much.

The discipline of prayer becomes a strategic act of interceding on behalf of our oikos, asking God to reveal His love to the people we share life with.

The discipline of generosity becomes a strategic reflection of God's grace, reaching out to our oikos in the name of Jesus with His resources (none of it belongs to us anyway), and then watching God draw them to Himself through the kindness of His people.

The discipline of service becomes a strategic foundation for ministry systems that fuel the church. Whether we care for infants in the nursery or hand out programs in the lobby, our efforts in serving provide support for others who are preparing to change their worlds for Christ.

Every time we are challenged to do anything as Christ followers, it is directly connected to our oikos. The high value of a local church is that it offers a place where believers actually become better prepared to be worldchangers. By growing in each Christian discipline, we deepen our relationship with God and reinforce our commitment to His mission to the world. In short, church helps! It helps us do our job!

DURABLE

For the past several years, HDC has engaged a restructuring strategy that reflects our analysis of recent American church history. Most of the churches enjoying dynamic ministry today were planted in this generation. Everywhere you look, virtually all of the great churches of former generations are now merely a shadow of their glorious pasts. The few who are experiencing new life are doing so only after an extended season of decline, culminating in a combative, albeit, inevitable hand-over of power to a new generation of worshippers. Our conclusion is that there must be a better way to perpetuate the effectiveness of the local church.

For years, our challenge was to build an effective church. By God's grace, that happened. Now, our challenge is to build a durable one. After all, why should a church family be asked to sacrificially pour significant resources into campus development, to only minister efficiently to that single generation, gradually die out, and then leave a large facility to service an ever-decreasing congregation? In fact, as we see it, durability is the essential component that is missing from current church-planting strategies.

The same principle, though, is true for individual believers. Our strategies for personal growth should allow us the opportunity to pass life's finish line with the same joy and enthusiasm that we had when we first came into God's forever family. Likewise, those strategies should include doing whatever we can to perpetuate our spiritual legacy for generations to come. In short, a local church will never be durable if the people who attend it aren't! Strong marriages, solid parenting skills, effective discipleship strategies—all are required to build a durable church.

We employ the oikos principle with that broad a vision, with future generations in mind—not just seeing the eight to fifteen people listed on an individual card, but how those ripple effects could impact hundreds or even thousands of people for generations to come.

ENJOYABLE

Joy remains the most attractive quality in the world. Conversely, grumpy believers and boring churches tend to be pretty good marketing tools for the enemy.

As the mother shook her young son back and forth, she told him in no uncertain terms, "Listen, we came to Disneyland to have fun and you're going to have fun whether you like it or not!" Well, I think that's a lot like many churches. People want to have a good time, but nobody really seems to know how.

Religion (which is no fun) has replaced relationship (which is)!

Churches seem to be working harder all the time to make their worship services warm, inviting and enjoyable. But what happens after the service is over is what really matters. Oikos still remains the most effective arena for expressing the joy that Jesus provides.

"May the God of hope fill you with all joy and peace as you trust in him, so that you may overflow with hope by the power of the Holy Spirit." (Romans 15:13)

What overflows out of your life to the people around you? Do you find yourself feeling like a hypocrite, trying to offer hope but feeling hopeless? Wanting to help others but desperately needing help yourself? On the one hand, we're all in the same boat—offering our world a perfect Christ from a life context that is anything but perfect. But the privilege of sharing in the redemptive plan of God is pretty exciting, especially since He really doesn't need us anyway. That's the primary attribute of God—self-sufficiency. In other words, God will never need anyone or anything outside of Himself to accomplish His will.

When you think about God giving us such an important role in the redemptive process, it does sound a bit counterintuitive. "Okay, Lord—You're going to come up with the genius of the Incarnation, make the herculean effort of the cross, work the miracle of the Resurrection and then leave the Gospel in the hands of a group of reluctant, easily distracted followers?" I mean, is that the best plan an omniscient God can come up with?

Evidently. And let me tell you why.

When my son was four, he asked if he could help me clean up the yard. I hesitated. As you know, I live in the desert—my yard was all I had to remind me that God had provided nature with a spectrum of other colors besides just shades of brown, so it was a big deal to me. People walking by would actually stop and say that our yard looked like a park. And, now, I'm supposed to partner with a four-year-old to keep it that way? I don't think so. But then I looked into his bright blue eyes, saw the anticipation and couldn't resist the offer. A two-hour job ended up taking four, but what the heck? I was being offered the chance to spend quality time with Drew, share life and accomplish something beautiful together? Who could ask for more?

I love the story Jim Kern tells about a game he pitched for the Texas Rangers. What had already been a tough evening got even tougher as he watched his manager, Pat Corrales make the long walk to the mound to pull him out of the game. Kern told him he wasn't tired. Corrales didn't flinch. "No, but the outfielders sure are." [2]

Jesus doesn't include us in His plan to change the world

because He needs us. I'm sure we at least double His workload, but He's hopelessly in love with us. He wants to spend quality time with us, share life with us, build up our confidence and give us significance—all the while accomplishing the mission He was going to fulfill anyway, to seek and to save the lost. Fly balls and line drives? No problem—He'll shag as many as He has to, just to keep us in the game.

"Change before you have to."

Chapter 16
A WORD TO CHURCH LEADERS

"I have become (Christ's) servant by the commission God gave me to present to you the word of God in its fullness." (Colossians 1:25)

The word "commission" (the older translations use the word "stewardship") is the Greek *oikonomia*—a compound term combining the now familiar *oikos* with *nomos*, which is Greek for "law." Paul's point is that God has been given each of us official (evidently, even legal) influence among that specific and relatively small circle of people. The English word accurately frames the intent of the statement—God's mission becomes our mission. We partner with Him to "co" that mission together! Any commission is unique to the individual believer but, as the Apostle to the Gentiles, I guess you could say that Paul's was "uniquely" unique. Our "co"mission is more "typically" unique.

My passion about emphasizing the oikos principle may frustrate some but I continue to insist that, if the Kingdom is to function on all cylinders, there must be synergy between Christ, the Church and the Christian.

• Christ died to save lost people.

• Christians are each given a "co"mission, a certain number of people they are responsible to point to Christ. In fact, Paul said in 2 Corinthians 5:19 that Jesus actually "committed to us the message of reconciliation."

• Local churches exist to facilitate strategic partnerships with local Christians, enhancing their success in delivering that message. Churches can misfire by not understanding their unique role. A great church finds ways to facilitate the Great Commission in the lives of believers who, quite frankly, don't feel that great at it.

THE IMPLICATIONS

It's one thing to tell your people to "go get 'em!" It's quite another to develop new ministry systems that will facilitate that process of preparation. If you want to be a part of an oikocentric church, the leadership of your church must consider the implications of that mission.

First, a pastor needs to determine how important oikos really is. The same thing is true with oikos as it is with every other aspect of your mission—leadership has to own it. But I can tell you from experience, a pastor can't just make it an oikos evangelism program. It won't be successful and then you'll blame me because it didn't work. Oikos has to permeate every discipleship element. It has to permeate every special event element. It has to permeate every worship service. It has to permeate every planning and strategy session. It becomes everything, even the only thing—because it's always been the main thing!

Earlier, I mentioned a group of pastors that I regularly meet with in San Diego. When we started talking about oikos, their excitement was initially tempered by the realities of ministry life—"If we were ever to make a commitment to an oikocentric ministry model, we'd have to get a few key leaders on board." So we set up a small meeting where they could each bring of few of their leaders and I could share the oikos model with them. I remember one of the guys saying, "I brought it up with one of the board members and he hated it, but he's coming to this meeting anyway as a favor to me." I reminded him of the necessity of his being fully persuaded first.

We spent a couple of hours together at that meeting and I think virtually all of them went away pretty excited about it. In fact, the board member who was expected to be the most skeptical actually became one of the most vocal supporters in the conversations that followed. You must convince your key leaders of its import, no doubt. And if this book can help with that, then I'm blessed to contribute something to the process.

Second, you have to commit to rethink every ministry system in your church. Jack Welch put it as clearly as anyone could—"Change before you have to."[1] Some of you are now scrambling for help because you already passed that threshold. But the core purpose of your mission and the core values you establish will not only support your restructuring strategies now, they will also be very helpful during seasons of future change. The negative emotion that often accompanies those conversations is mitigated because of the organic guidance those core statements provide.

Lastly, you cannot worry about over-emphasizing it. HDC hears about oikos in every service every single week. It is interwoven in the fabric of virtually every presentation we make. It's prominently displayed on what we publish. We talk constantly about keeping the main thing the main thing. In our membership class, I tell all of the participants, "If you're already tired of hearing about oikos, you're in big trouble! But if you can hang in there with us, we can change the world together."

LIVING IN A SMALL ENOUGH WORLD TO MAKE A BIG DIFFERENCE

We must never think so highly of ourselves that we start to believe that our churches exist for us. Both your and our churches exist for the people who don't attend them yet. But they will. No, really, they will! And they're not just going to come to our church, they're going to come to yours. And they will come because at some point you began praying for them. By name, by need, you broke out your card and took every one of them to the throne of God every day, asking God to reveal Himself to them. You invited them to church, not just once but a gazillion times, and they always declined. But you kept praying. Every day. Each one.

And God began working in their lives, revealing Himself to them in a new way. You didn't even know it, but a need began to evolve in their family that actually exceeded their fears and broke down their resistance.

And then one day you asked those same friends again, "Hey, we're going to church Sunday morning, do you guys want to go with us and then go out to lunch afterward?" And they said, "Sure." You thought you didn't hear them right, because they had always said, "No, we've already got plans." So, trying your best to hide the shock on your face, you clarified, "You do?" And they said, "Yeah, it's time we went along to see why you guys love it so much!"

So you went, together. They weren't intimidated by the new environment because you were walking up the steps with them. You knew the ropes. You showed them where the kids were supposed to go. You introduced them to the childcare worker and even to the pastor.

The service was what you expected, what the service always is—truthful, helpful and enjoyable. The Bible was taught. Principles for life were clearly communicated. The congregation was pretty fired up and joy permeated the entire campus.

All the way to the restaurant you were dying to ask them what they thought of the service but you didn't want to come across too strong, so you waited. But later, as the Diet Cokes were being passed around, you couldn't stand it any longer, so you asked, "What did you think?" And they said, "It was different. It sure wasn't what we're used to, what church was like for us when we were growing up."

You talked about the funny story the pastor used to introduce his message and how the guitar player looked like the guy who worked at the grocery store, because he *was* the guy who worked at the grocery store. And that was it. You called it a day, a very good day.

The next morning, when their name was next on your list you prayed differently. And the next time you asked them to join you, they readily accepted. And then again. And again. It was kind of funny to you because they talked to your other friends like it was their church now! They were even inviting people to tag along. And then one night about three months later, at the same restaurant, one of them volunteered, "You know that prayer the pastor prays at the end of all the services, that A-B-C prayer?" You said, "Yeah?" They continued in a broken voice, "Well, I prayed with him tonight and invited Jesus to come into my life."

And as you watched, everyone around the table broke out in tears and hugs and high fives. Then you sank back in your seat— and it hit you! And you thought to yourself, "This *is* the reason I'm here. This is my purpose for being alive." You didn't say it. But you thought it, and for the very first time, you knew it! Your life will never be the same because, from now on, impact is not just a pipe dream—now that you live in a world small enough to make such a huge difference, you'll never go back.

"Your focus need more focus."

Epilogue
MYTHS ABOUT OIKOS

Since this book was first released (under the title *Oikos, Your World Delivered*), we have had countless conversations with people around the world who desperately want to make a difference in their worlds. For many, this book has provided a first exposure to the oikos challenge and they've been taken in by its common sense logic. They are impressed by its biblical roots and cannot argue its impeccable track record. Yet some still find themselves pushing back against its simplicity. At the very least, your response might even reflect my own initial reaction—"If it's such a big deal, why haven't I heard about it before?"

Those who find themselves uncomfortable with the oikos principle tend to default to one of three basic and very valid critical concerns. Each of these concerns has led to sometimes lively, yet always helpful conversations.

MYTH #1: OIKOS IS TOO EASY

"Shouldn't there be more of an effort to evangelize the world, some classes to take, meetings to attend; some sense of urgency to go out there on the street and call people to repentance—argue with them, if necessary, until they give up and surrender themselves to Christ? There has to be more to evangelism than inviting people to church!"

Cold evangelism strategies have always had their place in Kingdom work and that approach may actually be the call that God has placed on your life. But, as strange as it may sound, oikos is actually the more difficult worldchange model, requiring an infinitely greater commitment to the process. Cold evangelism is complicated, but it's not that difficult—find someone with whom you can share the plan of salvation, have as meaningful a conversation as is possible and then walk away, more than likely never to see that person again. Whatever it turned out to be—whether a conversation, a debate or an argument—when it's over, you certainly hope for the best and probably feel some level of satisfaction about the fact that you have just "witnessed."

Conversely, oikos is a simple strategy, but not an easy one—because witnessing goes beyond what we say to people. Jesus said that we wouldn't go witnessing, but that we'd be witnesses! Because of your oikos, Christ-like behavior suddenly matters. The success of your marriage suddenly matters. Being a good parent suddenly matters. Learning the Bible suddenly matters. Intercessory prayer suddenly matters. And all those things matter all-day, every day, because a specific group of people are not only watching you, they are already being influenced by you.

Having said that, it's important to understand that oikos isn't just about being an example to people and keeping your mouth shut. Oikos means that the people who are watching you will, at some point, also want to talk to you—so you better prepare to have something worthwhile to say. It is not just about inviting people to church, especially if the church an individual attends hasn't yet committed to be a partner in the process. And even if you attend an oikocentric church, what if the people you invite to church don't accept your invitation to attend? What if they just want to meet you at Starbucks and talk about faith? Either way, you better prepare to have something to say because dialogue may be imminent.

MYTH #2: OIKOS DISCOURAGES COLD EVANGELISM

Remaining prepared to share Christ with anyone, anytime is every believer's responsibility, regardless of who is or isn't inside an oikos. But the fact is, without at least two people's permission, no meaningful conversation ever takes place. (If you're married, you already know this). Cold evangelism experiences can be very exciting, but successful ones are rare because people seldom grant that kind of permission on the spot. As one who designed the relational universe, Jesus knew where permission was most likely to exist—hence His consistent encouragement to "go home to your oikos." What you don't find in the New Testament is Jesus saying to recent converts, "Now that you're saved, go out on the street corner and argue people into My Kingdom."

Years ago, I heard an incredible story about a guy who, while walking through an intersection in a large city, noticed a police officer directing traffic in the middle of the street. As he walked by, the man sensed the Holy Spirit prompting him to go up to the officer and tell him that God loved him. The man dismissed the impulse and kept walking. Haunted by the continued sense that he had been disobedient to the Spirit, he finally walked back to that intersection, up to the cop and said, "Excuse me, Officer, but God just told me to tell you that He loves you." Tears started to run down from under the cop's mirrored sunglasses. Traffic stopped. With a broken voice, the officer said, "I prayed to God for the first time in a long time last night and told Him that, if He was real, the least He could do was to send someone to tell me that He was there for me." Within a matter of minutes, the officer called for backup and then prayed to receive Christ right there on that street corner. When I heard that story, I was mesmerized, to say the least. It was one of the most amazing and powerful conversion stories I had ever heard. As the speaker closed his message to our group that evening, he said, "Now go out and witness to people!" So we were all looking for cops all week! (Some of you may have had so many traffic tickets that the Highway Patrol probably *is* your oikos!)

There's nothing wrong with these events. In fact, they can be as compelling as they are dramatic. But never forget—they're rare! The problem is that, when they happen, we put those testimonies on Christian television, write books about them or use them as the centerpiece of some sermon on evangelism and then everybody starts to think that's the way people normally come to Christ. But they don't—at least 95% of us didn't come to Christ that way.

"I have been reminded of your sincere faith, which first lived in your grandmother Lois and in your mother Eunice and, I am persuaded, now lives in you also." (2 Timothy 1:5)

This was not only Timothy's conversion story, it may be the most boring personal testimony ever written. What is interesting to me is that it sounds just like mine and probably much like yours. Some may have to exchange the grandmother and mother for a father or a friend or a coworker or a neighbor. But most testimonies are eerily similar to 2 Timothy 1:5! No drama. Just worldchange.

Let me suggest that, if you're a pastor, you conduct your own research. As the opportunity affords itself, in a congregational setting, ask those who received Christ because of a "cold" evangelism conversation to raise their hand. Then have everyone look around the room to see the few hands that go up. The last time I did that, in an auditorium of thousands, four hands were raised. Before you move on, be sure to affirm the legitimacy of those experiences, even emphasize the divine power those few experiences reflect. Then ask for the hands of those who received Christ primarily because of the influence of one or more oikos relationships. Then have everyone look around the room to see the hands that go up—it will be almost everyone in the room. (And the people who don't raise their hand probably didn't understand the question.) To recognize the difference should not negate the importance of spiritual conversations that occur between strangers, but it will establish the value of the oikos. Rather dramatically, I might add.

MYTH #3: OIKOS IS JUST ABOUT GROWING A CHURCH

Growing a local church quickly isn't the goal of this book. In fact, if you're a pastor and that's your desire, then here's a better strategy—ask your church to hire a better preacher! That may sound harsh but, in most cases, it's true. The problem is, they probably can't afford one and, besides, God called *you* there! The oikos model will grow any church, with any style of any size. But more important than that, it grows Christians.

Actually, intentionalizing the oikos principle won't grow a church nearly as quickly as flashy programs will. But programs tend to impress people who already go to church more than people who don't. That's why there is a crippling number of Christians in our culture who simply move across town to the local church that has the best programs, the best bands or the best preachers. But the math doesn't lie—if one church grows at the same time another church shrinks, then there is no net benefit to the Kingdom. Church growth is important. But Kingdom growth is the goal.

A FINAL THOUGHT

When young Dre asked Mr. Han to transform him into *The Karate Kid*, the kung fu master agreed. But, for most of the movie, Dre's lack of discipline kept him from becoming the champion that Mr. Han knew he could be. As the story evolves, their ongoing, often tense dialogue is summarized in one pivotal and climactic exchange. Mr. Han simply says, "Your focus need more focus." Dre responds by making the necessary attitude adjustment and eventually lives up to the movie's name. [1]

And therein lies the difference between the Great Commission and the Mediocre No-Mission! Christians who live up to the name they bear are able to lock in on the task at hand.

Jesus came to accomplish a very specific job—to seek and to save people like us, those who were lost. Jesus didn't come to feed people or heal people. He did both because He cared about them, but when He took off (and I mean literally) there were a lot of hungry and sick people still here. Jesus came with a specific focus and He accomplished a specific purpose. He left the Father, was born of a virgin, lived a perfect life, died on the cross to pay the penalty for our sin, rose from the grave to conquer death and then ascended back to the Father. He finished the job He came to do, and then He left. That's why we call Easter Weekend the Passion of the Christ! That was His passion. That was His focus. That was something that He and He alone could accomplish. Nobody could save the human race but Jesus. If He hadn't bothered to passionately focus on His unique mission, then something really important would have never been accomplished and we would all still have to deal with the consequences of our sin.

So it should not surprise us to discover that focus is the primary building block of His church's mission, the strategy that Jesus brought to the formation of the church. God calls us all to be involved in very specific tasks (as indicated by our spiritual gifts), to get together with other like-minded believers at a very specific place (we call it a local church), so that we can better prepare to do life with a very specific group of people (we call them our oikos). That's our world. That's the world God wants to change—through us.

Are you in? If so, you're going to have to listen to Mr. Han.

Your focus need more focus.

Oiko-homogeneity

If you're hanging out with a bunch of slobs,
then you have an...*OINKOS*.

If you're touring with the Jonas Brothers,
then you have a...*BOIKOS*.

If you're serving in the United States Navy,
then you have an...*AHOYKOS*.

If you're spending weekends at the lake with the same
neighbors, then you have a...*TOIKOS*.

If you're always having lunch with a group of
vegetarians,
then you have a...*SOIKOS*.

If you're spending a month with visiting relatives,
then you have an...*ANNOIKOS*.

If your group is working together to bring balance to
The Force, then you have a...*DROIDKOS*.

If you're hanging out with a group of fun-loving
friends,
then you have an...*OIBOIKOS*.

If you have a ministry in the Jewish community,
then you have an...*OIVE'KOS*.

If you're shopping with friends who buy an awful lot
of
food and really big TVs, then you have an...*OIKOSTCO*.

End Notes

Prologue
1 Weber, Stu, <u>Spirit Warriors: Strategies for the Battles Christian Man and Women Face Every Day</u>, Sisters, OR: Multnomah Publishers, 2001.

Introduction
1 Barnes, Rebecca and Lowry, Lindy, "7 Startling Facts: An Up Close Look at Church Attendance in America," retrieved from www.churchleaders.com, 2013.

Chapter One
1 Wolff, Hans Walter, <u>Anthropology of the Old Testament</u>, Mifflintown, PA: Sigler Press, 1996.

2 Reagan, Ronald, "Farewell Address to the Nation," January 11, 1989.

Chapter Two
1 Lasorda, Tommy (1981), retrieved from www.sportingnews.com, October 4, 2007.

Chapter Three
1 Gladwell, Malcolm, <u>Outliers, The Story of Success</u>, New York, NY: Little, Brown and Company, 2008.

2 Reiner, Dr. Thom, "Ten Surprises About the Unchurched," <u>Christianity Today</u>, November 10, 2004.

3 Flugleman, Harry (Studio Chief at Goldsmith Studios), portrayed by Joe Mantegna in *The Three Amigos*, 1986.

Chapter Four
1 Kawasaki, Guy, <u>Willow Magazine</u> interview, Issue 3, 2007.

Chapter Five

1 Collins, Jim, <u>Good to Great</u>, New York, NY: Harper Collins Publishers, 2001.

2 Willard, Dallas, <u>The Divine Conspiracy: Rediscovering Our Hidden Life in God</u>, San Francisco, CA: HarperCollins Publishers, 1998.

Chapter Six

1 Warren, Rick, <u>The Purpose Driven Life</u>, Grand Rapids, MI: Zondervan, 2002.

2 Drucker, Peter, <u>Management: Tasks, Responsibilities, Practices</u>, New York, NY: Harper & Row Publishers, 1973.

3 White, Walter, personal communication, March 18, 2010.

Chapter Seven

1 Kirk, James T. (Captain of the Enterprise), portrayed by William Shatner in *Star Trek: The Original Series, The Omega Glory,* March 1, 1968.

Chapter Eight

1 Richardson, Don, <u>Eternity in Their Hearts</u>, 1981.

Chapter Nine

1 Robson, George, retrieved from www.thinkexist.com/quotes

Chapter Ten

1 Rogan, Alex, portrayed by Lance Guest; Centauri, portrayed by Robert Preston; Grig, portrayed by Dan O'Herlihy in *The Last Starfighter,* 1984.

Chapter Eleven

1 McLeod, S. A., "Social Identity Theory—Simply Psychology," retrieved from www.simplypsychology.org, 2013

2 Aristotle, "Rhetoric Book 1, Written 350 B.C.," Translated by W. Rhys Roberts. Theology Website

3 Twain, Mark, retrieved from www.brainyquote.com, 2013

Chapter Thirteen

1 Crain, Andrew Downer, The Ford Presidency, A History, Jefferson, NC: McFarland and Company, Inc. Publishers, 2007.

Chapter Fourteen

1 Covey, Steven, Principle Centered Leadership, New York, NY: Simon and Schuster, Inc. Publishers, 1990.

Chapter Fifteen

1 Collins, Jim, and Porras, Jerry, Built to Last, New York, NY: Harper Collins Publishers, 1994.

2 Corrales, Pat, retrieved from www.baseball-vault.com, 2011.

Chapter Sixteen

1 Welch, Jack, Winning, San Francisco, CA: HarperCollins Publishers, 2005.

Epilogue

1 Han, Mr., portrayed by Jackie Chan in *The Karate Kid*, 2010.

Pastor Tom Mercer, the Senior Pastor of Victorville, California's High Desert Church, has learned the power of the oikos phenomenon. After twenty-nine years and leading a church from 150 to over 12,000 regular participants, he has also learned how to train people to understand it.

His messages are available free of charge at the HDC website (HighDesertChurch.com) and, for a limited number of engagements per year, he is available to train your leaders or even challenge your entire congregation to consider their purpose in the world.

Log on to 8to15.com, where you can contact Tom, watch a video in which he describes the need for oikos awareness, order additional copies of this book and browse through a selection of tools that can help you and your church implement the oikos principle.